POWERFUL PARENTING STRATEGIES
FOR CONNECTING WITH YOUR CHILD AND BUILDING A STRONG BOND

Connection B4 Correction

CARRIE KHANG

© Copyright Carrie Khang 2023 - All rights reserved.

The content contained within this book may not be reproduced, duplicated or transmitted without direct written permission from the author or the publisher.

Under no circumstances will any blame or legal responsibility be held against the publisher, or author, for any damages, reparation, or monetary loss due to the information contained within this book. Either directly or indirectly. You are responsible for your own choices, actions, and results.

Legal Notice:

This book is copyright protected. This book is only for personal use. You cannot amend, distribute, sell, use, quote or paraphrase any part, or the content within this book, without the consent of the author or publisher.

Disclaimer Notice:

Please note the information contained within this document is for educational and entertainment purposes only. All effort has been executed to present accurate, up to date, and reliable, complete information. No warranties of any kind are declared or implied. Readers acknowledge that the author is not engaging in the rendering of legal, financial, medical or professional advice. The content within this book has been derived from various sources. Please consult a licensed professional before attempting any techniques outlined in this book. By reading this document, the reader agrees that under no circumstances is the author responsible for any losses, direct or indirect, which are incurred as a result of the use of the information contained within this document, including, but not limited to, — errors, omissions, or inaccuracies.

❦ Created with Vellum

Contents

Introduction 1

Part 1: Starting Point

Chapter 1: We All Have Emotion.................................... 3
   Big Feelings in Little Ones 5
   Parents Have Feelings, Too......................................13
Chapter 2: Checkpoints For Paren.................................18
   Accept Who Your Child Is...19
   Parenting Together 22

Part 2: Parenting For The Brain

Chapter 3: Brain Development 31
   Understanding Brain Basics....................................33
   Why the Early Years Count......................................37
   How to Support Healthy Brain Development 39
Chapter 4: Building The Brain.......................................44
   Learning by Experience 45
   Why Attachment Matters...48
   Myths and Facts about Secure Attachment................51

Part 3: Disciplining The Little Mind

Chapter 5: Why Kids Don't Listen 57
   Reasons Kids Don't Listen......................................58
   How to Handle Disrespectful Behavior 61
   Tips for Better Communication................................63
Chapter 6: Your House, Whose Rules? 71
   Know the Rules 72
   1-2-3 Method..76

Chapter 7: Gentle Discipline……………………………………………………..80
   *If Gentle Discipline Isn't Working………………………………*82
   How to Stop Yelling at Your Kids 84

Part 4: Building Connection

Chapter 8: Know Yourself……………………………………………………… 93
   Understand Yourself as a Parent 94
   Are You a Good Parent? 96
   Poor parenting skills? 101

Chapter 9: Time To Connect With Your Kids ……………………… 106
   Filling the Love Cup... 107
   Your Body Language 113

Chapter 10: Connection Before Correction…………………………… 119
   We want to connect... 121
   Why Connection Before Correction 125

Part 5: Connected Family

Chapter 11: Become A Better Parent ……………………………………. 133
   Are You a Good Role Model?.. 134
   Parenting Mindset 139

Chapter 12: It's Not Too Late ……………………………………………… 145
   Parenting With Fewer Regrets 146
   Letters from Your Child.. 150

Conclusion…………………………………………………………………………..155
References 161

FREE BONUS

Get your FREE PRINTABLES now.
Get our NEXT BOOK for free.

Introduction

"You can't make me do it. I hate you." My son yelled at me, looking defiant with his arms crossed.

If this argument happened in the past, things would have been really bad. There would've been lots of yelling, crying, and even threats. I probably would've spanked him or told him, *"How dare you talk to me like that? Now, go to your room before I lose it with you!"*

But now, I parent differently than I used to. I'm equipped with more knowledge, and that's helped strengthen my relationship with my son. Life couldn't be any better.

Still, I know a lot of parents out there are where I used to be, stuck in frustrating situations.

Let's say you've just had a long day with your child. It started when you began to leave the mall. He threw a huge fit, screaming, *"I am not leaving unless you buy me this toy!"* The episode embarrassed you, and it took everything in you to ignore his tantrum, despite wanting to drag him out of the mall. Now, you're back at home, but the whining continues. No matter how much you plead for him to stop and what you do to appease him, the kid is (seemingly) hell-bent on making your day miserable.

Well, guess what?

His supposed plan is working because you now feel tired, frustrated, and very upset. So, let me ask – what should be your next move in this situation? Give him a time-out? Ground him? Or just send him to his room for a while?

You've probably tried each of these options at some point. Come to think of it, whenever your child does something wrong, don't you react the same way, every time? Have you asked yourself why you keep repeating this same cycle? Maybe you've considered handling things differently?

Now's the time to consider connecting with your child. Of course, you know what connection means, but you're probably wondering why I bring it up in this situation. You're probably thinking something along the lines of, *"Why would I hug a child who just screamed at me and told me I'm the meanest mom ever?"*

The truth is, a child acting out, throwing tantrums, and having meltdowns is one that longs for connection.

Really?

Yes, it's true. Believe it or not, your kid's intent isn't to make your life complicated or miserable. They simply feel disconnected from you, and misbehaving is their way of expressing themselves.

When you punish your child or distance yourself from them because of "bad" behavior, it only creates more room for disconnection. And that's not what any parent wants.

As a new mom, I was filled with many questions about my child's behavior and how he expressed his emotions. It got so bad that, at one point, I was scared I was losing it. So often, I would look at my child's reactions and wonder why he acted like that.

"Why isn't he like other kids? Those kids are behaving so well! Am I doing something wrong?" I often felt like I'm not doing things right as a parent.

In those moments, my inexperience led me to tell him to knock it off or sit in the corner of a room to get over the situation. These consequences were shortcuts for me. Of course, I didn't mean any harm to my child. I thought that a little bit of "tough love" was good for him.

But here's the problem with that type of thinking. When you resort to using tough love tactics, do you honestly expect your kids to take the time and think about what they did wrong? Are you expecting them to say sorry to you during those long time-outs? Do you really think your kids will seek solutions to their problems all by themselves?

One final question: Are you kidding me? They are just kids! They don't have the experience to handle this kind of thinking on their own. It should never be an option to leave kids to themselves because they've misbehaved.

You have to find an alternative solution, and this is where discipline comes in. *Disciplining kids means you're teaching them which behaviors are acceptable and which are not.* Keep in mind that discipline does not mean punishment.

I've seen many parents use old discipline methods with their kids and assume their children will be okay afterward. I can't really fault them for doing so because many people, including me, grew up with parents who weren't good at connecting. They didn't have a role model who displayed healthy ways for a child and parent to relate to one another.

Unfortunately, many of us fall into this category. Our parents raised and disciplined us the traditional way. When we have our own children, we see ourselves doing the same because we don't know any other ways.

Let's assume you could use a time machine to go back to when you were a kid. Would you want your parents to discipline you the way you are currently disciplining your child? I am guessing the answer is no!

I remember how my heart was constantly broken because my parents always believed it was my fault whenever something happened. They seemed to think this no matter whose fault it was when my brother and I had sibling squabbles. My parents always assumed I started the fight and gave me a timeout each time.

I often wondered why they were constantly scolding me and accusing me of making mistakes. *Why won't Mom and Dad take sides with me for once?* I thought. *Why won't they ask me about the situation without yelling?* If my parents had reacted how I wished, I would have felt their love. I would have tried being a better child. But unfortunately, they never reacted the way I wanted them to. I know my parents have always loved me, but when I think back to how they treated me, I realize they often failed to show that love.

What about you? Don't you want to raise your kids the way you always wanted your parents to raise you? Instead of always assigning blame, why not get your child to trust you first and understand that you're on their side? This way, they'll become motivated to follow your lead.

Researchers have suggested that to form a healthy and strong connection with our kids, we need five positive interactions to one negative interaction we have with them. Since we spend so much time scolding, correcting, nagging, and yelling at our kids, we need to spend five times as much building a positive connection with them.

But we are only human. Being a parent is one of the toughest jobs out there! Some days, all we can do is meet our kid's basic needs. On other days, it's more like a full-blown war to bathe them, feed them, get them to do their homework, and get them to bed early. It's even harder to maintain an encouraging tone while doing so!

We know the tantrums are a phase and that disagreements won't last forever. Still, at this stage, our kids are already causing emotional distance between us, making parenting unenjoyable.

Why I Wrote This Book

I remember the day I slapped my son hard on the back right after he said, *"I wish you weren't my mom."* Even thinking about it now, I feel the pain his comment caused me. It hurt my heart so much, and I couldn't control myself.

I responded with, *"What did you just say? I wish you weren't my son either. You're making my life miserable."*

In other words, I ended up saying things that shouldn't be said to any child. I was a mom in need of help. Leaving my crying son behind, I ran to my room and shed a few tears behind closed doors. Little did I know that I was slowly disconnecting from my dear son with our constant, emotional fighting.

I hate to admit it, but at some point, I adopted the discipline methods my parents had used on me. They got used to saying, *"Just a minute," "Give me some time," "I'm almost done," "Not today, my love," "I'm busy right now," "Can't you figure it out yourself?"* and *"Let's do it tomorrow."* I hated that my parents talked to me that way all those years ago, but there I was, doing the same thing to my son. What an unpleasant truth to realize.

It took me years to figure out how to build a connection with my child, but the effort was worth it! Looking back, I understand how helpful this knowledge would have been. I am writing this book with the hope that other new mamas and papas can avoid the mistakes I made while raising my son.

Connection looks different for every parent and child. It depends on many different factors. This book provides the information you need while teaching the necessary skills. And I promise to not use a judgmental approach! There is no one right way to form a better connection with your child, but in this book, I explain the ways that worked for me and many other parents. Of course, the ultimate goal is to live a meaningful and enjoyable life with your kids.

For years, I've studied, researched, and read countless books on parenting and kids' psychology. It wasn't easy at first because I had to undergo many trials and errors. I had to apply what I learned to my parenting style so I could figure out what works and what doesn't. Ever since, my life has changed for the better! I believe the connection with my son gets stronger now because I see him smile more, and there is less tension every day.

I've written this book using easy-to-understand terms to keep the information accessible. Inside, you will find practical strategies and techniques. The exercises are a significant part of your parenting journey, so be sure to complete each of them.

Even though parenting may prove difficult and can seem overwhelming at times, I know that you've got this! The information and resources I provide will make the process easier. By investing time into your and your child's relationship, you will see the results are worth it.

Before starting your journey, though, let's begin with a quick visualization exercise. I want you to imagine that your child is a flower. When you are given this flower, you don't get to choose what kind it is. However, it is your job to nurture the flower in a safe environment. You know that your flower is the most beautiful one out there, and you must give it your full support 24 hours a day, 7 times a week. With enough love and care, you will see this flower blossom into its full potential. Just like this flower, your child will reach their full potential thanks to your support.

We all want to raise a happy, healthy, and well-behaved child who respects us throughout the years. So, are you ready to start connection with your child?

If so, buckle up, and let's start this journey!

Part One

Starting Point

If you've never been hated by your child, you've never been a parent.
    - Bette Davis

Chapter 1

We All Have Emotions

"When little people are overwhelmed by big emotions, it's our job to share our calm, not join their chaos." - L.R. Knost

"*You're the meanest mom ever!*"

My son yelled at me as he slammed the bedroom door and stormed out.

These hurtful words struck a chord in me as I was left standing, unable to move. Within the span of just a few seconds, I was filled with not only sadness but also several questions.

"What have I done to deserve this hatred from my son? Why does he like hurting my feelings? Am I not doing enough for him? What more can I do?"

Before I learned about healthy parenting methods, I was at a loss. Each day, it seemed like nothing I did helped. My son had made up his mind not to listen to me. He wouldn't get out of bed without a fight. He'd yell whenever he felt like it. Even worse, he'd scream for hours if he didn't get what he wanted.

All of us were kids once. We parents have been in many of the same situations as our kids find themselves in today. But can you remember exactly how you viewed the world when you were very little? Of course, you can remember certain things, but can you recall how intense everything felt at that time? Try to remember what it felt like when you were a child. Doesn't it feel absurd to have cried for toys that your parents clearly couldn't afford? Don't you wish you could go back to doing nothing but playing all day?

You see, we've all been there; we've been in the same shoes as our kids. But now that we're parents and have our own kids to take care of, it's somehow difficult to understand our kids, even though we were kids once. How ironic! Being a parent is a whole different game than being a kid. Remember, kids are still just *kids*, and you have to remind yourself that no one is born knowing everything automatically. That's part of the fun of life. We get to learn things as we grow!

We all came into this world as blank slates. Whatever you know now was learned over the years. This means our parents faced challenges while we were growing up because they had to identify *what* to teach us and *how* to teach us.

To understand your child better, you need to start with their emotions – what emotions your child feels, where they come from, and how to deal with them. This way, when your child acts out, you know the cause behind it. And when you know why your child's acting a certain way, you can identify a better solution for the situation. This process helps us to understand our children's emotions. Of course, when you understand your child better, you can form a greater connection with them.

Emotions are the intense feelings you experience throughout life. While you cannot see or touch them, they are always present within you. They're waiting for someone or something to stir them up.

Emotions are an essential component of life, whether what you feel is negative or positive. They are what make you human. These feelings start developing immediately after birth. However, they increase and get more complicated in the final years of childhood and early teenage years. External help is needed to understand and manage them more effectively.

Big Feelings in Little Ones

Have you ever wondered why your kid finds it difficult to explain their feelings in certain situations? Here's an example. Perhaps your son is playing with a transforming robot car. While trying to transform it into a car, he pushes it so hard that the toy's car door falls out accidentally. He's confused and doesn't know how to fix it. What does he do? He starts throwing the robot against the floor. If there's no one there to explain how to put the car door back on, he's probably going to end up getting frustrated and angry. He'll probably also burst out crying.

In this situation, your reaction may be to blame your kid for overreacting. Their emotions might even trigger some unwanted emotions of your own!

But let's think about it logically. We all know it's not easy for kids to control their emotions. This lack of control results from their inability to find the words that truly describe the feeling they are experiencing. I am certain you've experienced excitement, frustration, sadness, nervousness, anger, embarrassment, jealousy, and worry at some point in life, right? If you have, why do you think your kid can't? After all, they are humans, too.

But again, you might be thinking, *"They are just kids. How can they feel anger to such a strong degree? They are still so young. What are they getting so frustrated about?"*

If you have thoughts like these, now is the time to get them out of your head because here's the truth: Kids feel the same way you feel. They have emotions running through their body just like you have in yours. The difference between you and your child is that you have the ability to express these emotions in a hopefully healthy and useful way. Since kids are young and still growing, it might be difficult for them to use words to describe how they feel exactly. When words aren't an option, they end up expressing themselves in other ways. They use facial expressions and body language, which take the form of crying, rolling their eyes, giving mean looks, throwing tantrums, and sometimes simply "misbehaving."

You might look at your kid and wonder how they've turned out like this. You know your child probably doesn't mean to act in ways you don't approve of, yet here they are. From the moment you welcome your little baby into the world, they start learning the emotional skills they need to express and manage their feelings. They pick up these skills from the people they come in contact with, such as you, their grandparents, other relatives, and caregivers.

Since you are the closest person to your child, you have the sole responsibility to help them understand how they feel and why they feel and behave in certain ways. Once they understand why they're feeling the way they are, you can show them how to manage those difficult emotions in better ways.

Big emotions can be overwhelming for everyone, especially kids. You may wonder why kids experience emotions more intensely when they don't have much life experience. The answer is simple – kids' emotions are more intense because they are still learning to regulate their emotions. In other words, they are too inexperienced to learn how to keep their emotions from overflowing and becoming unmanageable. Fortunately, you're right there alongside them to help them learn to keep their emotions from getting out of control.

Helping Kids Deal with Those Big Emotions

What is the greatest gift you can give to your child? In my opinion, the best gift is the ability to handle intense and overwhelming emotions such as anger, fear, disappointment, and excitement in *healthy* ways. You don't want your child to be laughed at in class because they get noticeably frightened whenever they're asked a question. Neither would you want to be called into the principal's office because your child had a fight with someone after they let their anger get the best of them. Sometimes, situations like these can be completely avoided with enough emotional management and forethought.

Unfortunately, there are just as many times when unpleasant situations happen that are somewhat inevitable. Examples include the family relocating, a toy breaking, or parents divorcing. It's especially in these difficult times that your children need your help the most.

None of us were born knowing how to control big emotions like sadness, anger, jealousy, and fear. Whether it's getting their favorite snacks, waiting for their turn in line, or a pet dying, kids deal with big emotions just like us. Even if the causes of their feelings may be different from ours, kids' emotions are just as real and valid as those of adults.

Watching our tiny humans deal with big emotions can sometimes be hilarious, such as when they open a gift they've been waiting for and are overcome with excitement. But we might also find certain behaviors caused by big emotions to be annoying. Our kids can react in ways that bring even the strongest parents to their knees. The behaviors range from meltdowns, tantrums, outbursts, and screaming. And, as luck would have it, many of these extreme behaviors occur in public settings.

Dealing with big emotions is important to living a healthy life, even as adult. If left uncontrolled, these emotions can lead to problems that may require the help of a psychologist. What about kids? They aren't immune to emotional troubles, either. They often struggle academically, physically, emotionally, and behaviorally. If your kid experiences meltdowns or angry outbursts frequently, that's a sign that they need your help.

But don't worry. Your kids can effectively manage their emotions in difficult situations with your guidance.

I want you to imagine that your child's emotions are like waves in the ocean. As parents, you need to be there for them and teach them how to ride the waves. Don't teach or correct when your child's emotions are running high. This won't be the best time. You need to wait until the wave has passed before you can teach them about emotional management strategies.

Now that we know how important it is to help our kids deal with big emotions, let's discuss how you can offer help.

- **Provide strategies**

Whether they're toddlers or older kids, your children are still growing and aren't experts yet in dealing with big emotions. So, what do you do?

You provide strategies.

Below, we discuss examples of common ways to provide emotional management strategies for toddlers and older kids.

I am guessing you've experienced a situation similar to this one: Your kids scream because they want to go to bed wearing their Taekwondo uniform or princess dress or basically anything except their pajamas. In your eyes, they are misbehaving, and you only focus on the tantrums. You forget that what your child is doing is communicating, and they don't know how to express themselves better. So, instead of scolding your kid, why not accept the behavior as normal? Then, you can respond by teaching your child what to do. This way, they will be less likely to throw a tantrum next time.

Be calm and give your baby space. Use those words they are struggling to use. For example, *"I can see that you want to wear this Taekwondo uniform and not your pajamas, and it's upsetting you. Why not calm down, and I will tell you how to make it better?"* When the tantrums stop, thank your child for calming down and explain to them that the uniform is meant to be worn during exercises. You can say, *"Touch this fabric. You can see that it's very thick and not light enough for nighttime. If you wear this, you won't sleep well. But your comfy and cute pajamas will make you sleep peacefully."* With this understanding, they'll be more likely to go to bed in the appropriate clothing.

In the case of older kids, their vocabulary is more developed, and they may have words to express their feelings. However, they may also choose not to use them. In that case, what do you do when they shut out the world to avoid you, and decide to play only video games? Or when they start acting out on their anger?

Some strategies you can provide for older kids when their emotions are about to boil over include asking them to do a puzzle, ride a bike, count backward from 100, or do jumping jacks. You can even join them in one of these activities to show your support.

Note that what works for your friend's child or your neighbor's child may not work for yours. You'll need to try different strategies to find out what works for your family.

Keep in mind that a strategy that works one day may not work the next, so keep a list of activities so you can offer your kid lots of ideas.

- **Set realistic expectations**

What gift do you want your partner to surprise you with on your birthday? We can't deny the fact that, despite not wanting to seem selfish, deep down in us, there is still that special gift that most of us want. We keep our fingers crossed and hope we receive that gift from our partner. But expectation is always different from reality, right? When we don't get that gift, we don't whine. Instead, we just accept reality.

But when it comes to your kids, why are your expectations so high? Kids will always act just like that – kids. You will end up frustrated and disappointed when you expect too much from them. Therefore, you should set realistic expectations when helping your kids manage their emotions.

For instance, it's normal for a two-year-old to cry because they don't have their favorite snack, so don't allow their expression of emotions to frustrate you. Don't tell your child to relax and act like a big boy or girl when what they need is your empathy. It's better when you recognize their *need* for your empathy. You can then take the right steps to process why they feel that way.

Even though you may want to comfort your kid and do everything possible to make them feel better immediately after they throw a tantrum, don't try to speed up the process. Sit down with your kid and have a constructive conversation about what has happened. Then, discuss a better way to react next time.

- **Give validation**

Now is the time to validate your kid's emotions. By validating your little one's feelings, you acknowledge that you understand the way they feel. Whether they are happy, angry, sad, or experiencing any other big emotions, your validation is needed. By giving it, you aren't correcting them, teaching a lesson, or trying to fix them. Instead, you are showing them you understand the situation from their perspective. You're also showing that you empathize with them based on the situation they're experiencing. Ensure that your kids know that it is normal to have intense emotions. Kids all feel and express strong emotions that make them throw tantrums, shut themselves in their rooms, and scream at the top of their lungs. Some kids' emotions may not be as evident, but that doesn't mean they don't feel strong emotions.

Imagine this scenario. You go to the store with your four-year-old, and they suddenly see a toy and grab it. They try to toss the toy in the cart. You do your best to remain calm as you explain to them that you didn't come to the store to get toys but groceries. As you try to pacify your child and even promise they'll get the toy on the next trip, they lose it. Immediately, they start crying, screaming, and kicking. They're throwing a tantrum right in the middle of the store.

In this situation, what would you do next? You might sternly tell your child to stop crying and to "shush." You might try to get them to stop so you can avoid embarrassment, as people are beginning to stare.

But here's the thing. Despite your child's actions, they aren't trying to make a scene at the store or embarrass you. Being denied that toy triggered big emotions, including sadness and disappointment, in them. Their tantrum was their way of expressing those emotions.

If you find yourself in such a situation, try validating your child's feelings, even if you won't be buying the toy. Hold your child close and make eye contact with them as you explain to them that buying a toy wasn't part of the plan. Calmly inform them that you only have enough money for groceries, something that's even more important than a toy. You can also add that you'll plan for the toy and get it on your next trip to the store. This simple act can be very helpful to your child's emotional well-being. On your next trip, ensure that you keep your word. Kids will *always* remember everything you say, especially when it comes to buying toys.

* * *

Parents Have Feelings, Too

I understand how exhausting it can be to go back and forth with your kids about everything. These tasks range from making them eat dinner, getting them into the car for school, and convincing them to take their bath before bedtime. Not to mention getting them to adhere to screen time rules!

You probably ask yourself questions like:

"Why do we always start and end our day with a battle?"

"Why won't he just listen to me and do what I ask him to do?"

"How can a four-year-old cause me so much stress?"

Of course, you're tired of the battles. Your emotions are valid. Don't downplay your feelings or bottle them up because you don't want people to see you as a "mean" parent.

Do a quick Google search, and you'll read thousands of stories from parents revealing how they used to cry behind closed doors or in the shower. They'll talk about how they put on fake smiles so they can appear to be strong parents.

How do you deal with your feelings if you have kids that sometimes make you sad or hurt? What about when their behavior makes you feel discouraged, possibly even causing you to regret that you brought them into the world? Fortunately, there are ways you can cope and overcome your intense emotions.

Here are two options to try:

- **Don't take it personally**

Can you remember the last time your child got angry over what you said? What was your reaction? Did you scream back or talk calmly? If you say things like, *"How dare you say that to me? What is wrong with you? Don't make me lose it with you! You are such a spoiled brat!"*, then you are probably taking your child's behavior personally.

How do you feel when your child acts in ways you don't approve of? For example, think about when you call your child's name, and they ignore you. Or when you tell them to do something and they scream, *"I don't have to listen to you!"*

Some parents can respond peacefully by changing their reactions and addressing the situation with calmness. They can use a different tone, posture, and attitude. However, if you're the type whose buttons can easily get pushed, you likely think your child is out to get you.

The difference between these two types of parents is that one tends to take things personally while the other doesn't. Know that by taking your child's behavior personally and responding to it with a reaction, you're accepting their criticism and accusations. In a way, you're telling them you believe what they've said about you. For example, when your child screams, *"I hate you!"* or *"You're not the boss of me!"* and you react angrily, their words might be triggering an old memory of a time when you were bossed around and felt powerless. As a result, that feeling of powerlessness resurfaces and makes you react rashly to your kids.

When you fall into this trap, it's easy to assume the worst of your child and form misconceptions about why they disobey and disrespect you.

Even though saying and doing something this hurtful to parents seems wrong, don't forget that you're dealing with a child. This child hasn't learned how to regulate their emotions. Expressing their emotions by misbehaving is their immediate and natural response to what you did or said (or what they think you did and said). Don't take their actions personally. Focus on their behaviors, not their feelings about why they did it.

Of course, it's difficult to be unbothered and remain calm about such situations. This is your dear, sweet child we're talking about! Still, remind yourself that your kid is only a small human that is still growing and learning. They will understand their emotions soon, so don't take it personally.

- **Don't sweat the small stuff**

Don't get me wrong. I'm not suggesting that you ignore your child's

behaviors and leave them to themselves. But, if you keep punishing them for everything little thing they do, you'll definitely lose your mind.

Ignore the small stuff and pick your battles. Conversations that include sentences like, *"Put it back here," "Eat this," "Don't eat that," "Sit here,"* and so on are usually the ones that aren't worth battling over. You will burn out quickly if you keep lecturing your kids nonstop for every little thing. If they've made a mess, instead of fussing over it, you can clean it up later. I know it's very hard to look at a huge mess they made and pretend it isn't a big deal, but you need to keep your cool, at least for training purposes.

Your kids are growing and have *so* much to figure out daily. Letting little stuff go while you teach them to learn from their bigger mistakes is fine.

Kids think parents are robots who have no emotions and feel nothing. But hey! Don't let them keep assuming that. The next time your child makes you feel bad, tell them, *"Mom/Dad have feelings, too."* You can also say something like, *"You know, that really hurt my feelings."* This way, your kids will learn that you have feelings, just like they do.

Parents experience so many negative emotions. These include feelings of resentment, anger, deprivation, exhaustion, and many others. If they're not addressed, these feelings will consume and possibly destroy us. To fight the effect of these difficult emotions, we need to take care of ourselves. Otherwise, anxiety and depression can really take a toll. Please set aside time to take care of yourself. It's good for your emotions and your family's happiness as well.

> To be a good parent, you need to take care of yourself so that you can have the physical and emotional energy to take care of your family. — Michelle OBama

Chapter 2

Checkpoints for Parenting

"Every child is a different kind of flower, and altogether make this world a beautiful garden" - Anonymous

Let me guess: You were like me and got a lot of parenting advice before and after having a baby. Some of the advice was outdated, like when someone suggested using a dresser drawer instead of a crib. Other advice was hilarious, like when I was told to "Enjoy every moment." I wondered how that was possible. After all, I couldn't count the number of times I struggled with my son as he screamed in the toy aisle because he wanted a new truck.

But I can't deny that I've also been given good advice. Certain advice helped calm me and guide me through the daily challenges of raising my kid.

What is the best parenting advice you've ever received?

While you think of yours, here is mine: "Parent the child you have, not the child you wish you had." This advice hit me hard when I first heard it. I realized I was focused on wishful thinking. I compared him to other kids and always wondered why he couldn't be like them.

In this chapter, I discuss why acceptance is essential. I also talk about co-parenting with your partner or someone else.

Accept Who Your Child Is

Have you ever looked at your child and wondered what tree they fell from, and why they are so different from you and your partner? You might wonder why they didn't turn out the way you expected.

The truth is, many parents wake up and realize that their kids are different from what they envisioned. The little math genius you expected to have hates schoolwork. That sweet child you dreamt up disappears when it's time to have a bath and go to school, replaced by one that yells. The dreams of running around the park have faded because you have a child who throws tantrums and cries whenever you are out together.

So, how do you strike a balance and ensure that you are a good parent to your child and enjoy your parenting years regardless of what happens?

The foundation of every loving parent is **acceptance**!

What does acceptance mean to you, and what are you willing to accept about your child? Most parents say they accept their kids, but they really only do that to a certain level. You need to accept your child for whom they are, doing away with your earlier hopes and expectations of your child. Don't forget what unconditional love entails. It comprises showing love for your kids, regardless of what happens. It means not withholding your love for them due to certain conditions and honoring your kids for their existence in your life.

Don't expect your kids to prove anything to you before you show them love and affection. Your kids shouldn't be pressured to be a certain kind of person before they deserve your love. Neither should they try to live up to your expectations of them. Allow them to be who they are; their presence alone should be enough.

I've heard many parents say they love their kids and that their affection would never change, no matter what their kid does. But I've seen those same parents face a few challenges and take a step back. Suddenly, unconditional acceptance becomes a struggle. Being a parent means you should raise and celebrate the kids you have now, not the ones you were *hoping* to have. That means you should do away with those initial expectations you had for your child and embrace the child you have now. Accept all their faults, pains, strengths, weaknesses, embarrassments, tantrums, likes, and dislikes.

Our kids don't exist to make their parents feel good about themselves. They are unique beings and shouldn't be used to fulfill our dreams and ambitions. Instead, they need to feel our warm embrace and acceptance for who they are. You need to convince them that you love and accept them unconditionally. This way, they're less likely to feel overwhelmed due to our many expectations. This acceptance needs to be seen at home and outside the home.

Even though kids' behavior can sometimes be annoying and frustrating, you need to respond in effective ways. Think about how your reaction to their behaviors changes the way you communicate with your child. If you don't see things from their viewpoint and understand how they take in information, it might cause miscommunication. The result is that you feel like you and your kid are speaking different languages. As a result, you'll find yourself wondering, *"How is it that I'm saying all the right things, but this child keeps getting it all wrong?"* The truth is, the lack of connection between you two is causing miscommunication, and that means your child can't change their behavior.

As a parent, ensure that you find out what your child's "language" is; know what they understand and use it. If you don't, you may be missing out on connecting with your child. She won't understand the message you're trying to convey. If there isn't an effective way to communicate, you may not form a strong bond with your child. Communicate as much as you can in the right way, and set clear expectations and consequences accordingly.

Acceptance is essential in parenting. It will make you feel good about yourself and the child you are helping shape. Without acceptance, you'll find it difficult to parent a child who is navigating life and learning from their mistakes daily.

Parenting Together

Parenting can be challenging to do alone, so when you have help from your partner, you should gladly take it. Your partner's help should reduce the burden of responsibilities you have to deal with.

When raising children, it's important for both parents to work together as a team, and consistency in parenting is crucial. However, it's also important to accept small differences and disagreements with your partner while still maintaining core values. Core values, such as honesty, respect, responsibility, empathy, and love, are essential in shaping a child's character and behavior.

However, despite having shared core values, parents may differ in how they interpret and apply them in real-life situations. For example, suppose a child misbehaves at a family gathering. One parent may believe in disciplining the child firmly, while the other may prefer to take a more gentle approach. These different approaches may stem from their upbringing, personality, or beliefs about parenting.

Before my son was born, I barely argued with my husband. Everything seemed peaceful, and we had a tremendous understanding of everything. But after my son's birth, we began to argue over the smallest things like whether to breastfeed or bottle-feed, what his sleep schedule should look like, when the lights should be turned off and on, how much screen time he should have, what outdoor activities we should do as a family, what food he should eat, when he should do his homework…

If you are experiencing a similar situation, know that you aren't alone. There are so many parents still having arguments about these things, and many others. Even now, my husband and I still have different opinions about parenting my teenage son. But thankfully, it wasn't as difficult as it was in the early days.

But on a serious note, I used to get so angry with my husband because I thought he was doing things wrong. I felt like I was nagging when I tried to make him see my reasons. My happy home soon became a home full of arguing, and we gradually drifted apart. It was sad to watch.

The following are examples of conversations the two of us would have when we experienced different opinions about our parenting style.

Example 1

Me: *J (my son) doesn't want to play piano. It drives me crazy every time I have to drag him out to go practice with his piano tutor.*

Husband: *If J doesn't want to do it, you don't need to force him. Can't you just stop sending him?*

Me: *What? Why would you suggest that? If we keep allowing him to be by himself and have his way, what will he do in the future?*

Husband: *Why keep forcing him to do what he doesn't want to do? Your plan is going to backfire.*

Me: *Is the piano class for me? No. It's for J. He'll be thankful he learned it eventually.*

Husband: *Yes, it's for you. You want to have a son who can play piano.*

Me: *Stop saying that! I don't want to hear it anymore.*

As you can imagine, I got angry and raised my voice. I felt terrible, and we didn't talk to each other the entire day. My thoughts raced. *"Why doesn't my husband think like me? Doesn't he know that I want the best for our son? Why must we quarrel over every little thing?"*

Like many parents, my husband and I want our son to love and enjoy music, but we can have different opinions on how to apply them in practice.

Example 2

Me: *When are you coming home?*

Husband: *I'm not done with work yet. We are about to have another meeting, and I won't be home until later.*

Me: *What is that supposed to mean? Are you the CEO of your company?* (I said this in a sarcastic tone.)

Husband: *Come on, don't say that. Do you think I want to stay longer here? I feel tired, just like you.*

Me: *You are never home to help me. I'm always the one being both the mom and dad to our son. I am tired of it already!*

And again, another disagreement started from this conversation. It's not uncommon to feel this way when you're doing most of the parenting responsibilities yourself. The situation inevitably feels unfair and you're likely going to be angry. This anger can even affect your innocent kids.

Working as a team with your partner doesn't imply that you will never disagree. Of course, you will! As humans, we'll always have different opinions, experiences, ideas, values, and personalities. Let's not forget that you're *both* coping with the stress of parenting your little one. The stress will take its toll on both of you.

> Coming together is a beginning.
> Keeping together is progress.
> Working together is success
> - Henry Ford

According to scientific evidence, kids with parents who complement each other's differences are encouraged to be well-rounded and more open to trying new things. For example, one parent may be the rough-

and-tumble sort while the other is a gentle creative. They can use both qualities to help the child grow to become daring and artistic.

Over the years, I have grown as a parent. I've had to take a step back and ease up on many things. For example, I used to step into situations when my husband was having a serious talk or disciplining our son. Without realizing it, I took over the situation.

Initially, I felt I was better at parenting because I'm the one who's always around our son. I'm the one who reads more parenting books and the one who is always talking to parenting experts. I also spend more time around my son.

However, what this does to our kids is confuse them. Having two people give different instructions at the same time causes parenting disharmony. I was also indirectly undermining my partner, suggesting that he wasn't capable of teaching or raising our child.

You need to understand that parenting is a partnership. Trust your partner to give your kids the best parenting they can.

Your partner is different with their own unique characteristics

Keep in mind that your partner is different from you and will deal with life's challenges in their own way. Once you admit this fact, you will notice that parenting with different personalities exposes your kids to a variety of ways to cope with life as they grow.

Having unique personalities isn't a bad thing. We can't all be the same after all, and why would we want to be? You just need to find balance. If you continue to interrupt your partner's parenting style, then you're stopping them from practicing their parenting skills. Your partner needs to learn what works and adjust appropriately to improve their parenting, too.

Kids are resilient

I know it is difficult to keep still and watch when you know of a more effective way to handle things or when your child displays certain behaviors, but it's important that you don't interfere. You need to trust that your partner won't mess up your kid's upbringing because they do things differently. Remind yourself that your partner isn't trying to ruin your kids. They are only different and handle things differently from the way you would.

Thankfully, kids are resilient. Being resilient means your kids can learn from setbacks and manage their emotions better when they face certain adversities from your partner. Even if some situations aren't favorable to your kids, they can learn to contain their frustration, anger, and disappointment instead of acting on those emotions.

Talk it out with your partner

There's no perfect parenting style since every kid is unique with different characteristics. Meaning there will be times when you face challenges. I try to be intentional when I approach my husband and say, *"We need to figure out something that works."* I don't make it my problem but *our* problem. I use "we" and "us" instead of "I" or "You." When I want things to change or a new adjustment to be made, I make it our problem to solve. This way, we get to figure out the things we want to change together and avoid any confrontations about how we do it.

Parenting is a shared responsibility, and you and your partner are a team. Solve issues together. You can't always control what your partner does, and you'll find your parenting journey more fun and enjoyable if you're on the same page on major decisions.

Remember that parents are humans, and we all make mistakes. Instead of getting mad at your partner for not doing things the way you want them to, think about the times you've made mistakes.

Channel your energy into talking things out and finding common ground.

Parenting with your partner and accepting their parenting style teaches your kids the importance of family and bonding. You get to connect with your kids on a deeper level and prepare them for life.

Part Two

Parenting for the Brain

The best thing that you can give to your children is TIME

Chapter 3

Brain Development

" You never fail util you stop trying"
- Albert Einstein

Did you know that certain snakes eat their eggs when they're hungry? Yeah, I know. Pretty weird. You might be wondering why snakes would do such a thing, no matter how hungry they are. The truth is, not all snakes engage in this cruelty. The snakes that do it eat their eggs because they have weaker and smaller frontal lobes. As a result, these snakes have a limited capacity for emotions and work only for survival.

Thankfully, as humans, we can go a step further. Humans can feel all emotions and have brains that can process things more logically.

Did you know that your and your kid's emotions are controlled by the brain? It's amazing to know that your baby's brain is developing right there inside its tiny head, creating its emotions. You'll understand your kid's emotions and behaviors better by learning how the human brain works.

As embarrassing as it may seem, I didn't know anything about kids' brain development until I started reading books about it a few years ago. After learning how a kid's brain worked, a thought lingered in my head. *"Wow! If only I could turn back time, I would go back and spend more time and effort on my son's brain development."*

You might be wondering why I mention the concept of brain development when this book is supposed to be about connecting with kids. Well, there's a good chance you're like my former self. You probably haven't paid too much attention to your children's brain development. You might even have the misconception that kids' brain development is innate, and there is nothing left for you to do. While you don't need to know every little detail about how the brain works, having a basic understanding will make a significant difference in your parenting experience so you can connect better with your child.

This chapter is an easy-to-understand guide to your child's growing brain, with helpful tips to support their development. As you read, you will discover useful information and be awestruck by your little wonder all over again. However, note that I am not a medical doctor, a Ph. D. holder, or an expert in anything related to this field. It has been through lots of research that I've gathered the information relevant to this chapter. The information you will find here is accurate and based on reliable resources, so it's a good start for under- standing the concept of the brain without going deep into anatomical detail.

But first, let's discuss how the brain works.

Understanding Brain Basics

Did you know despite being so small, your baby's brain is made up of 85 to 100 billion tiny building blocks called neurons? If you wanted to count these neurons one by one, it would take years and lots of patience to finish. Amazing, though, right?

The human brain is a complex part of the body. Like a mansion, it has different "rooms" or components, including parts for listening, thinking, feelings, processing memories, and more. Your ability to effectively carry out tasks is a result of the connection between neurons of different parts of the brain. Brains can change over time, and it's easier to alter a kid's brain. This is good news because it means you can help your kids by being the superhero who helps them develop into their best selves.

Right from birth, our kids use their everyday experiences to develop their brain connections. These connections form when they have positive interactions with the people closest to them. Typically, this is their parents but can also include grandparents and other caregivers.

Kids use their senses to interact with the world, and their daily experiences will determine which brain connections they develop. These connections can last a lifetime. Now, you're probably starting to understand how important it is that your kids get all the quality care, interactions, and attention they can get from you at an early age. This will make a huge difference in their life.

The relationship you have with your kid significantly influences their brain development. It's essential that you build a loving relationship with them. While parents are whom kids should depend on, other dependable adults like teachers, caregivers, and other members of the community can support the child, too.

Kids give adults clues that let them know they want engagement with their parents or primary caregivers. Babies express themselves by smiling, cooing, or crying. Toddlers, on the other hand, communicate their needs more directly, often with words or emotions. Any of these modes of communication allows you or the caregiver to be responsive to your kids' needs.

When you give attention to your kids by responding and interacting with them often, you're helping to build their brains. This is why doctors always advise parents to talk, read, sing, and play with their kids from birth. These actions give kids the opportunity to explore the world. Interacting with your child also creates a safe and nurturing environment for your family.

The Brain's Basic Parts

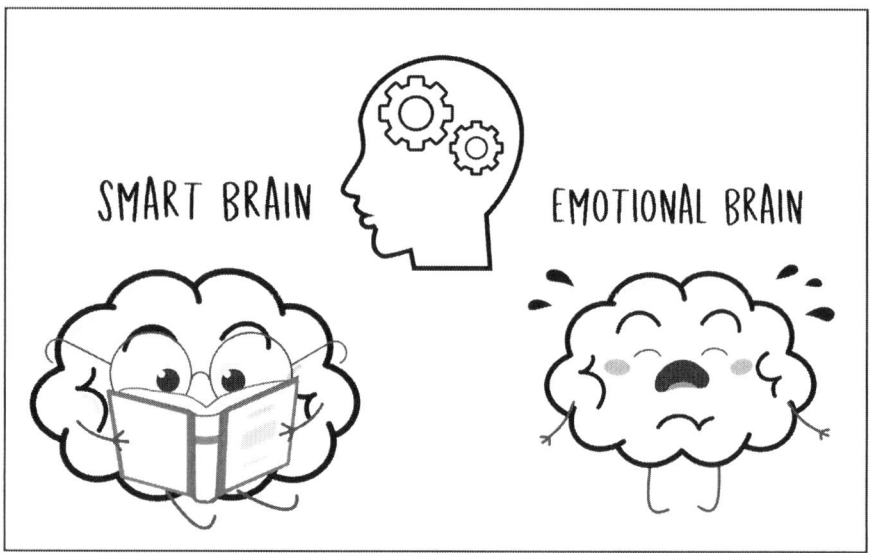

The brain is formed from two main parts: the emotional brain (limbic system) and the smart brain (prefrontal cortex).

- **The Emotional Brain**

The emotional brain plays a key role in managing and regulating emotions and processing memories.

Your baby's brain should be 50% of an adult-sized brain by age one. What should you expect when their emotional brain is fully developed and active?

This stage is when your baby will stick to you the most. They'll constantly crave your attention. For example, your baby will always want to be next to their mommy. When the daddy returns home, they push their little legs as fast as possible to get that first hug from their daddy. If they feel they are not getting enough attention, they start crying and throwing tantrums.

This is the stage where you will be doing most of the talking. You'll also be doing a lot of correcting behavior, cleaning up after them, and hiding just about everything from your baby. A combination of factors may lead you to frustration at this point. Your baby is seeking extra attention, throwing tantrums, pulling out everything in sight, wanting to always be next to you, crying, and never giving you a break.

This stage is when we hear parents complain about their kids, saying, *"I can't ever take a break. I wish I could rest a little, even for a moment."* You will likely feel like your child is different from others, and that thought might trouble you.

This is the point when you need to slow down and remind yourself to think positively. Your baby is only being what he or she is – a baby! You need to understand and tell yourself that your baby's emotional brain is rapidly developing, which is their way of building a lasting bond with you.

Kids with a developed limbic system have enormous social demands and many emotional connections. You might feel your parenting job is way too draining, and you don't have time for yourself. Remember that your baby needs this time and attention to grow and develop their brain.

If the emotional brain formation fails to develop properly at this stage, your child may ultimately find it difficult to regulate emotions and interact with others.

We have seen in the news that people turn into killers and commit murder without blinking, and some of them even look proud and without remorse. In many of these cases, it has been discovered that poor emotional brain development in early childhood resulted in severe and irreversible effects when these criminals became adults.

Being present in your child's early life is very important. If your child's emotional brain is not fully developed, it is not easy to finish the process later. The attachment between a child and their caregiver greatly determines how well-developed a child's emotional brain will be or if the potential will be wasted away.

A child's experiences shape how their brain grows. When stimulated positively, the brain forms a resonance related to those experiences and memories.

- **The Smart Brain**

The prefrontal cortex is located at the front of the brain. This is referred to as the personality center, thinking center, or smart brain. It helps us think about things, practice self-control, solve problems, pay attention, make decisions, and control big feelings.

Your baby's rational brain begins to grow at age three. After that, they get *very* smart. At this stage, you should be careful of what you do around them since they will likely pick up all your actions and imitate you.

Their smart brain develops by asking a long string of never-ending questions. They assertively say no to convey their feelings and make them clear. When they're told to do something, they usually reply with "No" or "Why?" to everything.

Do you remember your child going through that stage of answering "No!" to everything you said? Even when you didn't ask a question? I know how annoying and frustrating that can be. If you are experiencing this situation now, don't panic. It's only a phase. You should take your time to explain to your baby how to do things the right way. You can also tell them the right times when they should assert their tiny authority.

Why the Early Years Count

Even as newborns, children are born with tons of neurons. Connections between the neurons are reinforced depending on the type of stimulation they have with you or their caregiver. Examples include being held, talked to, and spending time together.

Your child's early years mark a significant period of their development, a time when their brain develops rapidly and forms connections and experiences. They learn and grow at an accelerated rate, and it is a time when they are receptive to new opportunities.

Are you familiar with Albert Einstein's childhood? Let me tell you what many people don't know about this genius. When Einstein was a child, very few people, nobody really, predicted that he'd be recognized as a great scientist one day. No one thought that a child whose speech was delayed would make remarkable contributions to science.

But what if I told you Einstein's parents had something to do with him becoming great? Something life-changing happened when he was 5 years old. While Einstein was sick and in bed, his dad gave him a compass that sparked his curiosity in science. Additionally, Einstein's mom, a professional pianist, gave him a violin. These gifts challenged Einstein's brain in different ways. Note that the focus here isn't the compass itself or the violin. What's important is that Einstein's parents gave him things that constantly stimulated his brain development.

The most critical phase of brain development in kids starts around two years old and ends around age seven. During this time, their brain learns faster, and their experiences have a lasting effect on their development. Parents must focus more on building healthy brain development for their kids at this point because it's the prime time.

Consider your child's early years as the best opportunity to improve their ability to build connections, be healthy, and become successful adults. Other higher-level abilities like self-regulation, motivation, effectiveness, and problem-solving are also formed in these years. If it isn't formed at this point, it can be postponed until their teenage years. However, we can't deny that it's harder for important brain connections to be formed later in life.

Therefore, seize the time now and start spending more time interacting with your little human to encourage positive experiences. The interactions you provide can build the architecture of your kid's developing brain. When you build a sturdy foundation from the start, you will have a good foundation for building a lifetime of better overall health.

The more you understand your child, the better relationship you will have with your kid. Ensure you know why your kid's brain development is important in their early years and provide support when needed. Since brain development happens sequentially, timing is important.

How to Support Healthy Brain Development

Helping your kid build a healthy brain may seem complicated, but don't be discouraged; it is a gradual process you can learn. Endeavor to see parenting as more of an art than a science. You can learn it on the job, even without a formal class.

Here are ways you can maximize your kid's early years and support healthy brain development:

- *Play*

Spending more time with your kids, especially during their early years, helps develop their brains. You might not know this, but your little one's day-to-day experiences significantly impact brain development. Through play, their ability to learn and solve problems improves. So does their academic performance.

Playtime can take the form of a game, singing, and other activities that can actively engage your child's brain. There are so many fun games you can choose from, including peek-a-boo, card games, the wheels on the bus song, building blocks, and imaginative play. Each of these types of play can trigger creativity in kids.

As you play with your kids, they'll pick up skills, learn new things, and grow physically, emotionally, and mentally healthy. They'll grow into adults who can effectively communicate and form relationships.

- *Nutrition*

As the power engine of the human body, the brain is always busy working. Therefore, you need to fuel it with the right nutrients to function correctly. Nutrition is essential for brain development as it influences how kids process and learn information. To give your kid's brain a good dose of fuel, you'll need to feed them with nutri- tive foods like eggs, blueberries, fish (with healthy oils), cabbage, chia seeds, soy, and avocado.

These foods are delicious to many of us, but you know how kids can be when it comes to trying new foods. They may not accept certain nutritious foods at first. If this is your case, don't worry. It only means they're not used to these new tastes yet. Allow them to try it out several (six or seven) times. Over time, they'll get used to these nutri- tious brain foods.

When the brain and the rest of the body are adequately fed, the brain will develop well. Your kids will grow healthy and intelligent. Ensure you feed your kids properly with a balanced diet.

- *Physical Touch*

Just like parents feel stressed, kids can feel stressed too. You might be thinking, *"What chores do they do that makes them stressed?"* Well, they run around the house and exert energy when playing, laughing, or even crying. Whenever you see your kids stressed, please don't leave them to themselves.

Let your kids know that you are there for them and that you will comfort and help them when they feel stressed. Studies have shown that increased physical contact helps kids feel comfortable and safe. When next you see your child looking sad, hold them close. Give kisses and hugs and encourage them to talk about what's wrong.

- *Read*

Often, reading is a skill that's overlooked by parents at first. It's understandable, as they are more focused on their child's physical well-being. But we can't forget about their mental well-being in the process.

We know reading is a vital ability to have in this world. Despite knowing the importance, I know, as busy parents, we find it difficult to create the time to read books to our kids. It can be more convenient to entertain kids with electronic devices, just so you can enjoy a few minutes of peace as you distract them from their tantrums. Please remember that expo- sure to electronic devices from an early age isn't good for them. I know it's convenient, but being convenient is not always good. Instead, foster a love of reading in your kids by showing them picture books.

When kids see pictures and hear words, it sparks their curiosity, and they want to know more. Expose them to reading books. Over time, they will recognize a correlation between what you say and the images they see in the book.

You can ask them to point to specific pictures in the book to support their learning. For example, you can ask, *"Can you show me where the ball is?"*

Better late than never

Hey, look... you're a powerful and wonderful parent. Don't feel overwhelmed by the information we have learned so far. You may not know how much influence you have over your child's brain development now, but trust me, you do. Your actions speak louder than your words, with each thing you do, you're stimulating some part of your kid's brain.

No doubt, we all know your kids can't hide from the genes you may have passed on to them. They are born with them. However, the environment you provide for them will determine whether your child will live up to their potential.

Before now, were you aware that a child's brain develops more from birth to age five than at any other time in life? I imagine some of you are sighing and feeling like giving up because your child is past five. You think it's already late. Please don't give up because it's better late than never! There is still hope. Your child's brain development will continue until they are a young adult!

So, if you're feeling a sense of doom because you feel you've missed out, there's no need. Our parents raised us without knowing all this information, and we turned out fine, so the situation isn't *that* bad. Don't get me wrong. I am in no way suggesting that you should follow in your parent's footsteps and raise your child exactly as they did!

Consider the cultural difference between our parent's time and now. Things are a whole lot different. People used to have large families with lots of interactions and play. But now, most families are small, unlike in old times. A different approach to parenting is needed.

BETTER LATE THAN NEVER

Chapter 4

Building The Brain

"Children learn as they play. More importantly, in play, children learn how to learn." - O. Fred Donaldson

We now know a child's brain is a wonderful organ that starts developing in their early years. But how can you ensure that your kid's brain is well developed and healthy, functioning at its peak throughout their life?

Let's compare building your kid's brain to building a house. The foundation of a house is critical. It's where every other component of the building stands. If the foundation is weak, it will affect the entire building. This can lead to the house collapsing later on. The same goes for your kid's brain. The brain development of their early years is essentially your kid's foundation, and you need to construct it right. The four walls of our example house represent your kids' emotional, social, cognitive, and physical development. When these areas are well developed, they also help make the house stand safely .

Remember, a house can be built with materials such as stones, wood, bricks, straws, and mud. These different materials have different strengths, and some are more durable than others. What are the durable materials you need to build your child's brain? Experiences! Kids learn through the things they see, touch, hear, smell, and taste. Then, they engage those same five senses to learn from their experience. With each repeated experience, the connection in the brain becomes stronger, and your child will to build confidence and competence.

Learning by Experience

"Use it or lose it" is a phrase many of us know all too well. Unfortunately, the expression applies to a lot of things, including brain development.

We've discussed how early childhood is a period when kids undergo massive brain development. The more stimuli a child experiences, the more connections form between neurons. This activates specific parts of the brain and strengthens existing neuron connections. Eventually, weak or unused connections are eliminated. This aspect of brain development is called synaptic pruning. This is the brain's way of removing connections in the brain that are no longer needed.

Have you ever tried your hand at gardening? For instance, maybe you've taken care of the bushes and fruit trees in your yard. If so, you're already familiar with the concept of pruning. Gardeners do this to encourage better plant growth and improved fruit taste. Pruning is essential to the gardening world for great, healthy results. Similarly, your brain prunes its neurons to cultivate a healthy brain.

Here is another example: Imagine your brain is an electrical outlet. What do you think will happen if you plug too many appliances in at once? They will likely overload the outlet, causing it to short out. Just like you prune trees to make them healthy, unplugging appli- ances you aren't using is beneficial to your electrical outlet.

The same concept applies to the brain. Shedding old and weak synapses you no longer need allows the brain to be efficient as you get older and learn complex information. It gives room for higher-quality connections that support complex mental functions. Synapses can be strengthened or weakened depending on how often they're used. The frequently used ones are strengthened, while the less commonly used ones get weakened, and eventually, pruned.

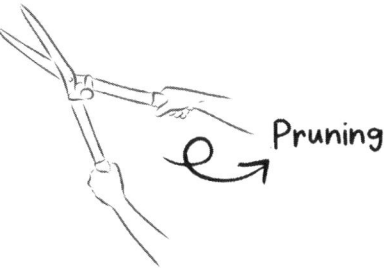

When you learn a new language, the pathways you use strengthen. But if you stop learning the language, your pathways responsible for that function will fade away, allowing others to be used. This doesn't mean you can't learn a new language again. It just means it won't be easy like it was during childhood and adolescence.

Depriving kids of emotional and social nurturing during this phase can seriously impede the developmental process. This is where you come in. You can influence the healthy development of your baby's brain and cognitive processes. The best part is that you don't need special equipment or toys to do this. What you need to do is easier than you think!

Connecting at home

We learned your kid's brain grows faster in the first five years of their life, and their early experiences influence their brain's physical development. This is why parents need to make the best of this period and help build their kids' brains. It all starts at home.

- *Make It Social*

You don't need to break the bank to buy the fanciest toys or go on expensive trips to make your relationship special. Did you know that you're already doing critical work just by interacting with your child? Yes, your kids learn best when they interact with you. You're the closest person to them. They trust you as their parent, so they'll likely believe what you tell them.

How do you make your relationship with your child social? Ensure you engage in a series of interactions with your child, even as an infant or toddler. With so many things to do daily, it can be challenging to make time for constant interactions. Try to interact with each other as you engage in different activities with them. For example, when cooking, you can explain what you're doing while they watch. Of course, they'll be too young to help much at the moment, but the aim is to identify opportunities for interaction.

- *Create Routines*

When you create routines with your kids, it makes them feel comfortable and safe. Kids are more likely to play, learn new things, and explore when they know what will happen, such as with a routine. Try to create everyday rituals even if you can't do certain things at the same time daily. For example, you can sing rhymes to your child when bathing them. You can also listen to calm and soothing music while you read them a book before bedtime. There are lots of other fun routines you can do together, such as exercising!

- *Follow Their Lead*

Remember how excited you were when your parents seemed interested in your paper planes? Or those times your parents cheered you on during a sporting event in school? Now, your kids need the same (or even more) support from you. When you see your child expressing interest in something, ensure you follow their lead and show your support.

By following your child's lead, even for just a few minutes, you encourage their curiosity and create playful moments between the two of you. Sometimes, you'll notice that your child can't do everything on their own. Allow them to explore on their own and don't take over. By letting them "fail," you're supporting their learning.

As I always say, there's no perfect parent anywhere in the world. Fortunately, you don't need to be perfect. All you need to do is be a good parent. That's the key to positively shaping your child's brain development process.

Why Attachment Matters

Attachment is a deep emotional bond with your child. Your child is attached to you since you provide most of their care. Do you remember that strong connection you felt with your baby immediately after birth? That same connection you've felt to your child all this time, they've felt for you, too. This attachment occurs throughout their development.

Attachment involves two people. While you respond to your child's needs, they will respond to yours as well. Over time, you'll realize how easy it is to comfort and soothe them. Even from a distance, they can easily react to you. You can promote attachment by rocking, holding, and talking to your child often.

Your baby becomes attached as you respond to their needs warmly and consistently. Attachment builds whenever you hug, feed, talk to, or play with your kid. It also forms as you go about your everyday routine with your baby, positively caring for and interacting with them.

Be aware that attachment can be a form of security or insecurity, depending on how the primary caregiver attends to a child's needs. But for this book, we will focus on secure attachment and why it's important to build that with your baby.

If you're always available, nurturing, and responsive to your kids during their first year, they will likely form a secure attachment. Although it may not be obvious at this early stage, you'll eventually see the impact later.

When a baby feels overwhelmed, the brain triggers the release of cortisol, the stress hormone. At that moment, if you respond positively and soothe the child, that will reduce the hormonal release and, thus, the feeling of stress. Likewise, consistent, positive responses from their primary caregiver teach a child to learn how to regulate their emotions and behavior.

Over time, neural pathways will build to enable the child to automatically self-soothe during moments of stress. Eventually, the child will learn to calm themselves when they experience uncomfortable emotions, such as anger and disappointment.

Now that you understand why attachment matters in a child's development, what can you do to support secure attachment between you and your kid? Let's say you are walking side by side down the street with your three-year-old, and suddenly, your child trips and falls. What is your first reaction as soon as you hear a cry? Do you wait for the child to get up on their own, or do you immediately grab them and check if they're okay?

I've asked a few parents this question and received different opinions. Some parents said they wouldn't help the child get up because they want them to develop independence. But that reaction is a no-no. All parents should quickly grab their children and care for them.

Your immediate response lets them know they can trust and depend on you for comfort and security. As you become more intuitive at interpreting your baby's way of communicating their needs, their attachment becomes even stronger.

Babies need to know you're there when they're sick, distressed, or upset. The best way to show your baby they're safe and cared for is to respond immediately to their cries. This does not mean you're spoiling the child. It's impossible to spoil a baby.

To promote secure attachment in your child, follow these tips:

- Be warm, responsive, and consistent.
- Respond immediately to the child's physical and emotional needs.
- Soothe the child in times of distress.
- Engage in regular play.
- Have positive physical contact (hugging, holding, etc.).

Myths and Facts about Secure Attachment

Having a secure attachment with your child is essential. However, this principle is often misunderstood by many parents. I don't blame them for their confusion because there are so many opposing opinions on the internet. It's difficult to separate what's true from what's not. In this section, I'll share a few common myths about attachment.

Myth 1: "I find it hard to understand my baby's communication signals. **I don't know what my baby wants, and that means my baby can't be securely attached.**"

Fact: It's impossible to understand your baby's emotional needs all the time. As long as you notice the disconnect and attempt to fix it, the bond will grow stronger. Do this, hold and cuddle your baby every time she cries. Watch and listen to your baby, staying sensitive to what they need. You will ultimately connect better with your child.

Myth 2: **"I spoil my babies by always responding to their needs."**

Fact: The more you respond to your baby's needs, the less "spoiled" they get as they grow. Your immediate responses to their needs help

you form a strong bond with them and create trust and independence.

Myth 3: **"Secure attachment is a one-way process that focuses on responding to my child's cue."**

Fact: On the contrary, attachment is a two-way, interactive process where your child reads your cues as you read theirs.

Myth 4: **"I need constant physical contact with my child to build a secure attachment."**

Fact: Of course, touching can be comforting for you and your baby. However, this doesn't suggest that you constantly touch or carry your baby throughout the day to develop a secure attachment. Nonverbal communication like facial expressions, eye contact, body language, and tone of voice can help create a secure bond as well.

Myth 5: **"If my child is securely attached, they will always be happy and won't cry."**

Fact: Infants have only one way of communicating their feelings – crying. They do this when they are hungry, tired, and uncomfortable.

They do this even when they don't know what their needs are. A securely attached child will act the same. They will feel comfort- able expressing their needs and emotions the best way they know. However, when a child grows up and is insecurely attached, they may be quiet and withdrawn from you because they know their needs won't be met regardless of their cries.

When you can separate myths from what's true, you get a better idea of the right steps to take to encourage secure attachment.

Ultimately, a child's brain is amazing and will continually develop throughout the years. However, the early years are critical. The tips offered in this chapter will help you ensure your child undergoes healthy brain development at this vital time. This advice will also help you form a secure attachment with your kid that makes them feel confident in relationships later in life

We're all imperfect parents, and that's perfectly ok.
Tiny humans need connection, not perfection.
- L.R. Knost

Part Three

Disciplining the Little Mind

Discipline is doing what you know needs to be DONE, even when you don't want to do it.

Chapter 5

Why Kids Don't Listen

"Don't worry that children never listen to you; worry that they are always watching you"- Robert Fulghum

You've just got home after a long day at work. All you want to do is eat and relax, but you can't! Your kids left their clothes on the couch instead of putting them in the hamper. You talked to your child about this problem not just yesterday, but the day before, and the week before that. Now, you have to talk about it yet again. What do you do this time? Scream at your kid? Throw the clothes into the bin? Okay, those reactions are a little overboard.

You're not alone if you've experienced this situation or a similar one with your kid. Every parent has probably struggled with persuading their child to listen to them at some point.

My son used to put me through the same thing. I would come home every day and find a million and one things to complain about — the running faucet, dirty plates on the table, and scattered books across the sofa. The list was endless. I was frustrated, and my son was, too. Making the same request daily for him to keep things organized was very tiring.

I had a chart with colorful pictures of his chores pasted in his rooms. But that strategy didn't work. I went the extra mile to go over his chores with him every morning. That didn't work either. No matter how often I corrected him, he repeated the same mistakes.

My nagging made me feel like a bad mom, and self-doubt began to creep into my mind. My son was probably tired, and I was the villain in his life. It wasn't much time before I began to question my parenting skills. Was I doing something wrong? When did I make my first mistake? It took several weeks of self-evaluation and the constant support of my husband before I got back to feeling like myself. Over those few weeks, I discovered new ways to get my kids to listen to me and do what I want. I'll tell you what I discovered.

Reasons Kids Don't Listen

Children, though way younger than their parents, are humans, too. They have minds of their own. They feel the hurt and frustration of constantly being told what to do. Why, then, don't they listen to us the first time then? Why do they constantly make you repeat your requests over and over?

Let's find out!

The following are reasons why it seems like your child isn't listening.

- ***They didn't hear you.***

Contrary to what some parents think, children are busy people. Yes, busy, but in a different sense than adults. They're caught up in a world of their own. They have their own things to do, from homework to playtime to hanging out with friends.

Your child will probably not hear you speak if they're distracted by homework or are chatting with a friend on the phone. The next time you feel like your child didn't listen to you, don't assume that they're being defiant. Confirm that they heard you when you were speaking.

- ***They didn't understand.***

I once noticed that whenever I gave my son instructions, he would nod and say *"Yes."* Then, he would proceed to do something different from what I asked. I realized he had listened to me but simply misinterpreted my words.

No matter how old your child is — whether they're an infant, tween, or teen — they aren't as experienced as you are. They don't have the knowledge you do, and it might be difficult for them to understand some tasks. After stating your instructions, explain in detail what you want your child to do. For example, instead of saying, *"Josh, I want this house squeaky clean,"* say, *"Josh, I want you to dust the chairs, do the dishes, and scrub the floors before I get home from work."* This way, you've spelled out each task that should be done and how your child should do them.

- **They couldn't do it.**

When you give instructions to a child, you believe they can handle the task. But what if they really can't? What if the task is harder for them than you think it is? For instance, imagine you ask your son to move the play table back into the corner of the room each time he finishes playing. Each time you ask, he doesn't do it. You may see his neglect as a sign of disrespect. But what if the table is too heavy to move on his own? Sometimes, a child doesn't do what you ask because the task is more than they can handle. Ensure your instructions are age appropriate.

- **They didn't want to do it.**

Like I said earlier, kids have minds of their own. They have activities they love and activities they hate. Your child will most likely not listen to you if you've asked them to do something that doesn't interest them.

No one likes being told what to do. Not even kids! Imagine yourself in the following situation. You've been thinking about cleaning the bathroom. Suddenly, your partner asks you to do it since you're standing right there. If you're like many people, you might think your partner is ordering you around. The thought of your partner doing this is enough to make you bristle. Can you see your kids' point of view now? So please, don't scream at your kids or give orders. If you become too demanding or controlling, your kids will become defensive. They'll always be on their guard against you.

I'm not implying that you should let your kids get away with bad behavior. It's okay to guide your kids and train them to act responsibly. But don't exercise more control than necessary. Give your kids a break! Don't just assume your kids are stubborn. When your kids refuse to do something, try to identify the reason behind their refusal. As we both know, their behavior is their way of communicating.

How to Handle Disrespectful Behavior

Our children's disrespectful behaviors, such as ignoring us, yelling, refusing our requests, arguing, and name-calling, can be painful experiences for parents. However, this behavior is your wake-up call. It's a reminder that as a parent, you should be in control of the situation and that you need to set boundaries. Next, we'll discuss *how* you can handle disrespectful behavior from your kids.

- *Overlook Their Attention-Seeking Behavior*

As parents, you may think, *"Why should I ignore their attention-seeking behavior? Isn't that letting them get away with it?"* The truth is, you can't always respond to everything your child does. If you did, you would quickly stress yourself out. The most efficient approach is to select the things you react to. For example, if you ask your child to leave their plate on the kitchen counter after eating and they roll their eyes, don't react. Engaging in a power struggle with them means it will take longer for them to accomplish what you requested. Instead, remind them of the consequences if they don't clear their dishes. As for the eye-rolling, you can address the issue later, when you and your child are both calm.

At that point, you can say, *"You rolled your eyes when I asked you to put your plate on the kitchen counter after eating. Did you realize you often do that, and that behavior hurts me?"* Let them know it is disrespectful and makes you feel bad. Then, explain the consequences of disrespectful behavior.

- *Give Consequences*

Sometimes, kids' disrespectful actions may need immediate consequences. Consider their age and the severity of their offense to know which consequence to give. When your five-year-old screams at you, immediately let them know their action was not appropriate and provide an opportunity to correct it. If they fail to do that, you can follow up with a consequence. You can give them a time-out or restrict access to their iPad or TV. You can also tell them they won't be going on that playdate you had planned for them.

The right consequences actually motivate your child to demonstrate good behavior. This method puts you back in control and teaches your child how to problem-solve. When applied effectively, this method also gives your child the skills needed to be a successful adult.

- *Make Use of "When/Then" Statements*

Don't we all want to earn privileges in life? At work, many of us strive to do our best when we know something is at stake, such as a promotion or a bonus. Let's apply the same incentive to our kids. Instead of giving lengthy lectures on what your kids *can't* do, let's focus on encouraging them to change their behavior by using *"when/then"* statements. For example, you can say, *"When you allow me to finish my chores, then I will come into the living room to figure out why the TV isn't coming on."* Say this instead of something like, *"I will spank you if you don't allow me to focus and finish my chores."*

Talk to your child calmly instead of raising your voice. Let them know the importance of being kind and polite. The idea is to give your child a chance to change their behavior.

- **Use Restitution**

You can use restitution to encourage a disrespectful child not to let the behavior happen again. Restitution is something nice that's given or provided to compensate for any damage they've done. For instance, if your child hurts their sibling, you can make them do something nice for the person they've hurt. Or if they disrespect you, their restitution can be doing chores for you.

Let your child know that simply saying "sorry" won't always fix things. Instead, they should learn to take responsibility for their actions. Restitution will make them take responsibility and work toward repairing the relationship.

I understand that it can be challenging to deal with your child's disrespectful actions. Sometimes, you might try everything you can think of and still not see changes. But you need to also know that consistency is key. Even if you encounter setbacks, be patient with the process as you encourage a positive change.

Tips for Better Communication

Given our busy schedules as parents, we tend to keep conversations with our kids light. We often do this because we want to move on quickly to the next item on our to-do list. There are moments when casual talk is okay, but there are also times when your child wants you to focus on them and pay closer attention.

Here are four tips to help you communicate better when your child needs your full attention.

Avoid dead-end questions

Question: "How was your day?"

Answer: "Fine."

Questions: "What did you learn today?"

Answer: "Nothing."

Question: "Who did you play with during the break?"

Answer: "No one."

Does this conversation between a parent and child sound familiar to you? If yes, then you now know that you need to come up with better questions to ask your kids after school. Put yourself in their shoes. For example, imagine that after a long day at work, someone asks you, *"How was your day?"* You'll likely respond with a short answer, like *"Fine."* Why do you expect a different response from your kid?

I understand that, as parents, you may have a busy and exhausting life. It's hard to find time to be creative and ask questions that kids will find meaningful. It's not easy to come up with unique and interesting questions right away because we're so used to resorting to tedious and obvious questions. However, when asking your child questions, try to make them more specific and engaging. The questions will challenge their brain and give them direction when answering.

If you ask, *"How was your day?"*, your kid will most likely say *"Fine."* or *"Good."* And the conversation ends there. It's better to ask original, open-ended questions appropriate for your child's age. You'll get them to open up and have meaningful discussions.

What are open-ended questions? They are questions that cannot be answered with a simple "yes" or "no." They instead require the respondent to elaborate.

Mom: *"Did you finish your homework?"*

Child: *"No."*

Mom: *"What? Why not? (In an annoyed tone)*

Hopefully, this reaction is not the kind you have. The child gave his honest answer to the question his mom asked. Even though he told the truth, in cases like this, parents often get angry because it's not the answer they expect or want. But take another look at the question. It was a question that could *only* be answered with a yes-or-no response. And the mom's reaction was way stronger than the question warrants.

How about this question instead?

Mom: *"I heard you've got a lot of homework today. How is your homework coming along?"*

Child: *"I've done the first half, and I'll finish it after I'm done eating my snack."*

Mom: *"Great. Let me know if you need any help."*

Child: *"Sure, thanks!"*

This question requires a bit more explanation, not just yes or no. Depending on the exact question you ask your child, your child will have a different response. Keep in mind that if you're quick to anger, your child may lie to avoid getting scolded. Hopefully, that won't happen!

I found some fun questions to keep you and your child engaged in a conversation for holding a longer time. Of course, your questions need to be age and situation appropriate. Here are some examples you can use for talking to school-aged kids:

- *Did someone make you feel upset/happy today?*
- *Did someone make trouble during class?*
- *Who brought the yummy food to their lunch today? What was it?*
- *If you could have a superpower, what would you do in a class?*
- *What other ways would you run the class if you were the teacher?*
- *If you could make a class rule, what would it be?*

- *If you could teach any subject, what would it be?*
- *What was the funniest thing that happened to you today?*
- *If you could change something about your day, what would it be?*
- *If you could be invisible for a day, what would you do?*
- *What's the funniest word you know?*
- *Which 5 words do you think best describe you?*

Even when you ask good questions, your kid might respond with quick answers. If you experience this, don't be discouraged. Remember that Rome wasn't built in a day. Like most things in life, it's a process that takes time. Continue practicing your question styles with them, and you'll see that they will become more engaged as time passes.

- ***Don't lecture them***

When you say things like, *"Stop being so untidy,"* *"You're always doing this,"* and *"You never pick up your clothes,"* you're lecturing. Lecturing gives unnecessary information that reinforces your child's negative feelings toward themselves. Parents tend to stretch a ten-second response into a twenty-minute lecture! This is funny because it never does any good.

When you lecture your kid, you make it hard for them to listen to you. Their minds will eventually block out your voice. This means they'll start to ignore you, roll their eyes, or talk back. There's a good chance they'll even continue to act the way you don't want them to.

As much as you want to vent out all that's on your mind, don't! Just keep your calm and remain composed. Be as brief as you can when speaking to your children. This way, they won't have time to tune you out!

- ***Keep it simple and short***

Repeating your instructions makes you sound like a nagging mom or dad. You sound like a broken record that keeps repeating the same thing over and over. No new information is given. Just the same old crap!

If you can convince your kids to do the dishes with just three words, do it. You don't need to tell a story about how young you were when you started washing dishes. You also don't need to tell your kids how you were the only one in your family who did the dishes. Your kids simply don't care about that information! Talking too much gives the impression that you are unsure of what you will say next.

The best way to speak is to put your key point in the first sentence. Keep everything as short as possible, including how you want a task done. Remember, a single word or two will means more than a lecture.

- *Be mindful of what you say*

As parents, we are conscious of how our kids communicate with and react to others. We correct them as necessary and make sure they behave politely. However, we aren't always mindful of our words as parents. We often speak unkindly and reprimand our kids without mercy.

"You don't do anything right."

"You're so lazy."

"You always fail your tests."

Have you ever said these words to your kids? It's easy to get caught up in our emotions when we're angry. We become so furious that we say hurtful words to our kids.

Although these words are said in the heat of the moment, your words could scar your kids forever. Your child might become demoralized and start developing self-limiting thoughts like *"Maybe I'm a loser"* or *"I can never do anything right."*

When a child makes a mistake, it's important to help them understand that they did something bad, but that doesn't mean they are bad. It's natural for kids to feel guilty or ashamed when they make a mistake, but it's important to help them separate their behavior from their sense of self-worth.

Try to avoid labelling them as "bad" or "good" based on their behavior. Instead, focus on the behavior itself and how they can improve it. For example, instead of saying "you're a bad kid for hitting your brother", you could say "hitting your brother is not okay, let's talk about how you can handle your anger in a different way". This helps them understand that their behavior is what needs to change, not their sense of self-worth.

Be kind to your kid. Make your voice soft and calm, even if you're correcting "bad" behavior. They'll love you more when you show them respect and kindness.

Finally, saying *"Please"* and *"Thank you"* isn't something only young people should say. Use these words with your kids, and make it clear that you expect them to use these words in return. There'll be a greater connection between you and your child once you learn to treat each other with respect and love.

Chapter 6

Your House, Whose Rules?

"Without my children, my house would be clean, my wallet would be full, but my heart would be empty" - Anonymous

Your house rules won't necessarily be the same as those of your neighbor or your mom's friend. For example, while your sister might be comfortable with her kids running around the house and jumping on the sofa, you don't allow such in your home. Or maybe, while Grandma isn't okay with your kids using devices at the dinner table, you don't have an issue with it.

It's crucial that you create a set of rules for your household so your kids know what is and isn't allowed. By establishing rules, you aim to reduce misbehaviors and encourage consistency with discipline.

Setting rules for your kids can be way trickier than you think. When you set too many rules, you'll find yourself in too many power struggles. That's when your kids dig in their heels. You'll start hearing, *"Nope! I don't want to do that, Mommy!"* It can also make parents look like authoritarians barking orders at their kids all day long just to make them do what they want.

But can we parents really survive using only gentle parenting and no rules? Imagine a world without traffic rules. We'd all drive around chaotically. I know this example sounds extreme, but the aim is to point out how important having rules at home is. Rules are made to prevent something unhealthy or bad from happening. Without rules, our kids can run amuck, drive us crazy, hurt themselves, and make us feel frustrated. So, how can you create balance by being not too strict and yet not too loose with your kids? That's our focus in this chapter. We'll discuss how you can walk that fine line of not pushing your kids away but still getting them to follow your rules.

First, let's start with the first step!

Know the Rules

What are your rules? Now is the best time to identify and define your rules. If your kids are toddlers or preschoolers, you might want to start by setting just one or two rules. They're too young to remember many more. Start with what they can remember and give them a chance to learn those before adding others.

Also, avoid creating unclear rules. For example, when you say, *"Be good!"*, this instruction can mean different things to different kids. Why not be clearer by saying things like:

"Don't interrupt when someone is talking. Wait your turn to speak.'

"Always tell Mommy the truth."

"Don't jump on the furniture. It's meant for sitting on."

"Don't yell in the house. Use a calm voice."

Behaviors that are unacceptable to you should be stated clearly. For example, instead of saying, *"Don't be rude and cheat,"* you can say, *"Always wait for your turn when you're playing together."*

As your kids grow, they won't always be at home or preschool. They will begin to explore other places where there will be different rules. You won't always be at their beck and call to help them out. As much as following rules outside the home is important, following rules at home is equally necessary. The good news is that if you can teach your kids to follow the rules at home, it becomes easier for them to do the same in other places.

Your house rules don't need to be hard or complicated. However, always remember that these rules need to be followed because they'll direct your child later. Rules help them know what to expect from their surroundings as they navigate the world. When they've grown up following good rules, they'll become disciplined adults.

Ensure that your set rules are realistic. For example, don't expect a toddler to do things meant for older kids. For example, it can be difficult for a three-year-old to remain in their bed every morning or clear the table after eating. Set rules that are suitable for your child's age.

Keep in mind that your rules should apply to everyone in the house, even you. Yes, you! When setting rules for limiting TV time, don't say, *"No more watching TV after 7 p.m."* unless you plan to stop watching at that time, too. Lead by example, and set rules specific to your family's needs.

If you don't have your family rules in place already, pause for a minute and consider what you want them to be. Here are three suggestions:

1. **Keep yourself, and others, safe.**

Kids are so adventurous. They're always getting into trouble. They have a knack for hurting themselves by playing with hot things, throwing sharp objects around, and climbing to dangerous heights. But can we blame them? They're still learning how to navigate the world and need your guidance. This is where setting safety rules comes in!

By setting safety rules, you will keep your kids in check when they play with their siblings. It will also help them stay safe around adults, pets, classmates, and friends. Teach your child to be alert and proactive in unfamiliar situations. This way, they can remain safe even when you're not there. For example, it's important that you tell your kids never to give out their personal information to strangers. They should never allow anyone to touch their private parts and should always inform you if something like that happens.

2. **Be respectful to others and their property.**

Maybe I'm getting old, but it seems like the kids of yesterday had more manners and respect for people than today's kids. But, of course, we didn't have access to what they did back then. Still, my parents made sure to teach me to be respectful, polite, and have manners. It was a priority.

It doesn't matter if a family member is older or younger; respecting every family member is a non-negotiable rule. Name-calling, answering back, walking away rudely, slamming doors, and throwing objects in anger is disrespectful and should be discouraged.

Teach your child not to hurt anyone by pushing, kicking, or hitting them. They should always ask for permission to borrow other people's property. Finally, they shouldn't hurt anyone's feelings by name-calling, yelling, or putting someone down.

3. **Follow directions to create established norms.**

Kids can be dramatic. They often know the rules but don't follow them. Your child won't always agree with your decisions. Clearly state the rules to create established norms. For example, you can say, *"Take off your shoes before coming inside,"* or *"Make your bed before leaving for school"* or *"Brush your teeth twice a day."* You can explain to your kids why it's good to follow these rules by explaining the reasoning behind them.

No matter how angry your child may make you, please don't shout at them or make them feel ashamed. Instead, explain what is expected of them and how you only want to help them.

For rules regarding electronics, set a time to cut them off before your kid goes to bed. A screen cut-off time helps them establish a good sleeping routine. However, while some families limit their screen time to an hour or so per day, others allow the TV to be on for longer but turned off at certain times. It all depends on what works for you.

Don't forget to track your child's progress with following your rules. Make visual aids that will improve their understanding.

1 2 3 Method

It's one thing to set rules, and it's another to enforce them. You can use the 1-2-3 method to ensure your kids follow your rules. This is a simple technique that you can start using today.

The **"1"** represents the first warning. For example, if you notice your kids' toys aren't put away, you can say, *"I need you to pick your toys up after playing with them."* Allow a few minutes for your child to consider and comply with your rules.

The **"2"** represents the second warning, but this time around, it comes with a consequence. For example, you might say, *"I'm telling you again that you need to pick your toys up after playing with them. If they're still there in 3 minutes, I won't let you play with them for one week."*

The **"3"** is your last warning. It's another reminder of the consequences. If your child complies with the rules, thank them for doing a good job. They will be more willing to cooperate with you next time. If, after a while, your child remains unconcerned and their toys are still all over the place, you can pick up the toys yourself. Quietly put them away without making a scene.

If your child is disrespectful, curses, or calls people names, you can give out two warnings and establish consequences for your child. For example, your child could lose one hour of electronic time after your two warnings.

Note that safety-related behaviors such as being physically aggressive don't need two warnings before taking action. For example, if there's a situation where your child hurts their siblings or throws things at you, you can give a time-out and make them lose their whole electronic time for that day.

Look out for behaviors that don't need your response. Behaviors such as whining and complaining are the type you can ignore and shouldn't respond to. They can be considered a way to "stall" or avoid doing a certain task. However, if the behavior doesn't resolve on its own and it escalates to something more serious, you may need to remove your child from that environment. Avoid the situation until the storm passes. You can say, *"I know how upset you feel that I'm not giving you your favorite snack. Well, it's not a choice, and your misbehavior affects everyone here. Let's take a walk*

Remember, the 1-2-3 strategy can be done with minimal talking. We already learned from the previous chapter that lecturing doesn't help. Don't overreact or get too emotional about your kid's reactions. With the 1-2-3 method, you're giving them a choice three times with a warm and calm tone. Whatever option they choose, they will understand that the result is their responsibility, even when they don't like it. After a while, they will understand what it means to follow the rules, what breaking them means, and how they can be responsible.

While the 1-2-3 method can be effective for some children, it may not work for all children or in all situations depending on a number of factors, including the age and temperament of the child, the consistency and clarity of the instructions given. It is important to note that no single disciplinary technique works for every child or family, and that may be necessary to try different methods or seek additional support or resources. So don't be upset if this doesn't work.

Finally, when giving a warming, you can start by setting clear expectations and explaining to your child what is expected of them. Let's say a parent wants their child to clean their room regularly. First, don't expect the room to be sparkling clean, and instead of saying "clean your room," give them clear instructions like, "place books on the bookshelf and toys in the toy box, and empty the trash can. If something falls to the floor pick it up and put it back."

Once the child understands what is expected of them, parents could praise the child when they clean their room on their own, reward them for consistently cleaning their room, or simply thank them for their efforts.

If the child doesn't meet the expectations, the parent could provide a consequence that was already discussed with the child such as no video game for 2 days, no electronics for one day, or an extra chore.

It is normal for kids to break rules and test your limits. If they do this, don't be disappointed or give up. Like I always say, these are just kids. They're going to act like kids, so cut them some slack. On the other hand, if you experience opposition from your kids and rules get broken, consistently follow up with consequences. This way, you are teaching your kids how important obeying rules is.

Chapter 7

Gentle Discipline

"Children will listen to you after they feel listened to"
- Dr. Jane Nelson

Life can sometimes be like a big science experiment for our curious little ones. They are everywhere, snooping around and eager to know everything. But as parents, we can't always allow them to poke around and prod everything in existence. We need to be alert and keep them away from trouble.

Bigger kids are also innocent and naïve, and caring for them can be an overwhelming task. One minute they are screaming at the top of their lungs; the next minute, they are waking you up at 3:00 in the morning, asking for water, spitting up on their brand-new clothes, and doing all sorts of things that get on your nerves. But can we really blame them? They are just kids. However, what if they continue with those misbehaviors like getting into your makeup bag, splashing water in the dog's bowl, and chewing on everything they see? You definitely don't want to let them get away with everything. What's your best approach to discipline?

It's helpful to remember that there are no bad children, only bad behaviors.

Whether you're dealing with a naughty kid or a screaming toddler, you should never be in a position where you are extreme with punishments or resort to physical violence. These will only give a short-term result and never a lasting solution.

Let me introduce you to a better way of handling your kids. Have you heard of gentle parenting? If you have, what's your opinion about it? Have you tried using it?

Gentle parenting is simple! It is simply treating your kids like the little bundle of joys they are. With gentle parenting, there is no humiliating your kids because they want something from you and no scolding them because they made the living room a mess. You don't compare them to your neighbor's kids because they broke your favorite flower vase, and you don't give them long sermons about how you were treated when you were a kid.

These are just excuses and negative reinforcements that many parents use to control their kids. With gentle parenting, you can help your kids stay out of trouble. They're more likely to listen to you and their spirits won't be crushed.

If Gentle Discipline Isn't Working

Do you feel like gentle discipline won't work? Do you even believe you can parent your child without raising your voice or punishing them? Perhaps you've been nothing but sweet to your kids, and yet, they terrorize your life. Now, you've concluded that gentle discipline isn't for you.

I've heard parents who believe they practiced gentle discipline complaining about the approach, saying it doesn't work no matter how hard they try. The kids become destructive, aggressive, and defiant. Sadly, I've also heard stories of kids less than five years old who intentionally hurt their preschool classmates and others who simply seem angry at all times. They are like a walking time bomb, waiting to explode.

The common question among these parents is, *"How can my child act this way despite the fact I use a respectful and gentle approach?"*

Before I offer possible solutions, I must clarify a misconception about gentle discipline. Gentle discipline focuses on teaching kids appropriate behavior. You discipline gently when you avoid getting into a confrontation with your child instead of reacting rashly to your child. For example, if your kid hits their sibling, don't hit the child back or give an extreme punishment. Your child doesn't even know the gravity of what they have done. The right approach is to sit next to your child, hold their hand, and make eye contact. Calmly say, *"Don't hit your brother again because it really hurts. Imagine if he hit you. How would you feel? You're supposed to protect your brother and not hurt him."* This way, you're teaching your child to use kind words. You're also teaching your child how to express their feelings in socially appropriate ways.

Gentle discipline isn't about having your child get their way at all times. Of course, you can compromise on simple things, but show them a better way to act when it's serious. You may wonder, *"Why does everything sound so easy in theory? Does it really work?"* The truth is, while your strategy may not work at first, using the right approach to try again will work eventually. I totally understand your doubts because I've been there.

. . .

Connection

The truth is, your kids need to feel connected to you for gentle parenting to be successful. While laughing, hugging, and running through the grass with your kids come to mind, it is also crucial to stay connected during boundary setting, even if the situation doesn't appear warm and fuzzy.

You can connect with your child by:

Talking to your child: When talking to them, ensure you state your message clearly and use precise language. For example, when you don't want them to do something, you can say, *"I don't want you to do this,"* or *"I won't let you do this."* Statements like these are what kids need to hear first when they misbehave. They can instantly connect you with your child because you're clarifying your expectations. Children deserve respect and a straight answer from you.

Acknowledging and empathizing with your child: Children like it when their perspectives are taken into consideration. They want to feel heard and acknowledged before you set limits.

I know it may sound easy to do these things, but looking back, it's embarrassing to confess that it wasn't easy for me to even just talk with my son. I also found it difficult to acknowledge and empathize with him because I was so accustomed to getting angry right away when my son did something wrong. There was no room in my mind to talk to or understand my son's heart.

How to Stop Yelling at Your Kids

If you have a stormy personality like I used to have, you're probably quick to lose your temper. I bet there are times when you wish you had reacted differently.

I remember getting to a point where I felt like a loose cannon. I would yell at my son because I couldn't control my temper. Over time, I discovered my voice was at its loudest every time I talked with my son.

How did I ever get to this point? Good question.

I'm glad I learned how to be a better parent. I learned to never justify my anger or take it out on my adorable kid. So, if you are the type of parent who finds it difficult to control your temper, I will show you how you can effectively manage your temper and be a better parent to your little one.

But first, here's what I think about anger. I believe anger is a natural thing. And as humans, we are going to be angry at different points in our lives, and we have the right to feel that emotion.

Is it okay to feel angry? Yes! Feeling anger is acceptable. But it is *never* okay to lose control of your temper. Acting out in anger or losing control of your emotions and unleashing it on someone else (probably the one who triggered you) is not okay.

You could end up letting those bottled-up emotions spill out onto your children when you're angry, and that's never a good thing!

Before we get to the different strategies you can use to stop yelling at your kids, let me quickly clear something up. Never think yelling at the top of your voice, spanking your kids, or giving them extreme punishments will curb your kids' misbehaviors long-term. These actions might limit misbehavior at that moment, but they won't stop them in the future. Using extreme measures will teach your kids that it's acceptable for older people to be mean to smaller kids. It will also show them that it is okay to express anger through violence. Research reveals that extreme measures such as yelling and spanking can change a child's brain structure. I doubt that's what any parent wants.

Don't take your anger out on your kids, no matter how angry you get. Instead, use effective strategies.

Strategies for Controlling Your Temper

The following are strategies to help you control your temper so the next time you get angry at your kid, you can handle the situation better and feel proud of yourself.

- *Stop Yelling Over the Small Stuff*

"Close the damn door!"

"Drop it, and don't touch my stuff!"

"Do it now!"

"Don't touch that!"

"Put it back!"

"Just stop it!"

"Why won't you listen?"

Do any of these demands sound familiar? Do you get so hung up on the little things your kids do that you tend to reprimand them repeatedly?

Perhaps, you always tell your kids to sit up straight at the dining table, hold the fork properly, or clean up a spill immediately. But do you need to point out every little thing at the dinner table? Of course, dinner manners are important, but all they want is to enjoy their dinner.

The point I want to make here is that you don't need to call attention to every time your child behaves in a way you don't like. What is your priority, anyway? Is it having an enjoyable family mealtime or one that's full of complaints, tears, and nagging?

Even though your child's actions might be getting on your nerves, you have to let the small stuff go. Don't get yourself worked up over such unimportant things.

Your reaction and the words you use when angry are a result of your temperament and how you were raised. Even when you find it hard to control yourself when triggered, you need to. Find ways to control yourself and carefully choose what comes out of your mouth next. Don't say something you will regret later. It's definitely not an easy skill to learn, but it's something you need to do.

Most times, we react a certain way because we think that will get our kids' attention, and that yelling's the only way to do that. But let me ask this: When you yell at your kids, how do they react? Do they listen to you and immediately do what you've requested? I doubt it. I don't think your yelling works in these scenarios.

For insignificant problems, you can let them be. You don't have to bring them up each time they happen. Also, take note of the tone of voice you use when you do address a behavior. Remember, the tone of your voice matters a lot. Talk to your kids in a normal, calm voice. That way, they'll return that same energy to you. They'll stop yelling back with excuses when you call them out on something.

We want to teach our kids that expressing their emotions and feelings is okay, but it's not okay for them to yell at someone, hit others, or wreck things.

- *Use Parenting Affirmations and Mantras*

Affirmations and mantras can help you to stay on course toward your goal. That goal is to stop yelling and learn to control your temper.

Repeating an affirmation or mantra at set times will help you stay calm and remain in control of your emotions.

I use affirmations and mantras mostly in the morning after washing up. Doing this ritual at a set time will help you engrave these words and beliefs inside your mind until you subconsciously act on them.

You can stand in front of your mirror, look directly into it, and repeat the statement to yourself. After doing this regularly, the action will become routine and feel natural to you. This process really helped me, and I want every parent struggling with their temper to try it out.

Here are some of the affirmations and mantras I use before I go to bed, before I go out in the morning, and when my baby pushes my buttons. These statements help me find peace.

- *I can remain calm, no matter how my child behaves.*
- *My child is not giving me a hard time. My child is having a hard time.*
- *I can react better this time.*
- *I am a loving mom/dad.*
- *I love my child/children.*
- *This is not an emergency.*
- *He's just a child.*
- *I'm a mom, and they are just kids acting their age.*
- *I won't say or do things I will regret later.*
- *I want my child to feel happy, not frightened.*

- **Stop and Take a Deep Breath**

Sometimes, you just need to stop everything. Stop, inhale and exhale. You've heard so much about deep breathing and might wonder whether it works. *"How can simply breathing in and out make me feel calm?"* you're probably wondering.

Research has shown deep breathing can be a form of therapy that is very helpful in calming the mind.

At the very moment you feel triggered, instead of letting your temper overwhelm you or saying words that are hurtful and toxic, redirect your anger. When I feel triggered, I always take a big, deep breath in and let it out for a few seconds. Sometimes, I will also make a fist while thinking about why I am getting angry. I also think about my baby when he sleeps peacefully and how much I adore him. At that moment, all I want to do is hold him, hug him tight, and kiss him.

Breathing exercises can quickly slow down your rising emotions and soothe your temper.

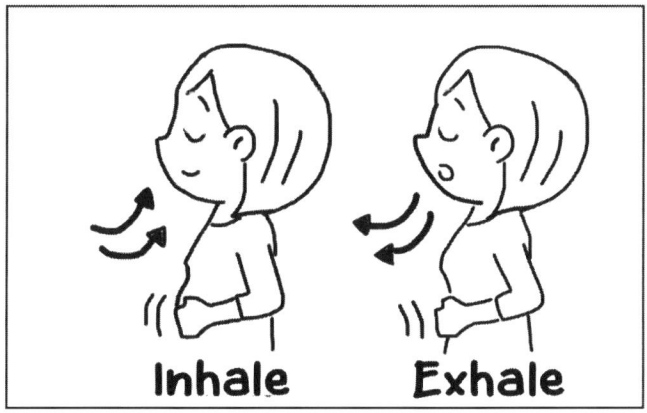

If you are still not calm after taking a few breaths, how about taking a walk? Instead of yelling, *"I need a break!"* you could say, *"I'm too upset right now. I need to calm down."* You could also recall your affirmations and mantras at this point.

- ***Tone Down Your Triggers***

Try and figure out when you get triggered the most. My early trigger was getting my baby to sleep when he was younger. When he started school, my trigger became weekday mornings. It was always a battle, and yelling never helped.

Kids are likely to mirror what they see. So, keeping your cool may mean they'll keep theirs, too.

I tried strategies to put a leash on my triggers. For example, I woke my son up with a kiss and a hug. He loved it. It made him feel relaxed and loved. It also helped him talk to me gently since he felt good in the morning. I started seeing great changes when I started practicing this morning routine. I also experienced fewer triggers throughout the day myself. Just imagine your partner giving you kisses and hugs, telling you *"Thank you for all you do for our family!"* before heading to work. How would that make you feel? I bet you'd be starting your day with a big smile, right?

Finally, giving your kids the right direction and enough affection will make them more willing to listen to you. It will also reduce conflicts and help form a better connection with your children. Sometimes, you might be tempted to treat your kids like they are your best friend. As parents, you should lead and teach your child as they grow. Disciplining them doesn't mean you're a mean mom or dad. Rather, you're instilling confidence in them. The lessons they learn from you will help them navigate life.

Disciplining kids is an ongoing process that requires work on your part. Put in the work, and you'll eventually become proud of your young champ!

Part Four

Connection

Kids don't need things.
Kids need parents who spend time with them.

Chapter 8

Know Yourself

"Do what you can, with you what you have, where you are."
- Theodore Roosevelt

Hey, parents! If I may ask, who exactly are you? I know this question may sound strange to you right now, but it is an important one. You'll need to provide an answer to really grasp the purpose of this chapter. So, let me ask again, who are you? What makes you tick? What makes you furious or happy? What are your strengths and weaknesses?

Once you understand who you are, you can then effectively control your thoughts, feelings, and actions toward your kids. Your personality embodies your behavioral patterns, traits, interests, attitudes, social roles, and emotional responses. Now that you have kids to care for, it's important that you know yourself better.

Knowing yourself makes it easier to figure out the things you need to fix about yourself. You'll be less anxious or stressed because you know where the problem lies and how to go about solving it. This chapter focuses on **you**! You will learn to pause, truly see yourself, and know what kind of a person you really are. In addition, you will identify the kind of parent you want to be. Knowing this will help shape the direction of your emotional well-being and parenting style.

Let's start by understanding yourself as a parent before we dive into the subject of connecting with your kids.

Understand Yourself as a Parent

I'm guessing you had many preconceptions when you learned you were expecting a baby. You already had hopes and dreams of how you wanted your kids to turn out and how you wanted to parent them. Sadly, not everything in life usually goes as planned. Certain things may get in the way of your plans.

Parenting isn't about perfection, even though we want to be the best parent we can be. We get blinded by our past, psychological struggles, and emotional defenses. These things can influence our parenting style, and we unknowingly create a rocky road for our kids when we're supposed to make things easier for them.

As parents who want to raise healthy kids with secure attachment, you need to look inwardly and understand yourself. You'll need to examine your beliefs, mindset, and own attachment style. When you understand these parts of yourself and where you stand on certain issues, you can make more sense of your life. You can come to terms with your past and help your child flourish.

From birth to childhood, your subconscious mind forms beliefs about yourself, how you see others, and the world. Your experiences teach you how to view yourself. They'll prompt your mind to determine whether you consider yourself good or bad. These experiences will also shape your beliefs about whether you deserve love or if you're undeserving of it.

We can't ignore the emotional baggage you may have from your past. You've got resentments, unhealed pain, severe losses, and fears from the past, and these issues still affect your present experience. These childhood experiences have helped form your mindset, core belief, and expectation of who you are and how you relate to your kids. When you don't know yourself well, you can be controlled by outdated beliefs which affect how you parent. Awareness, on the other hand, allows you to make healthier parenting choices that connect you better with your child.

As you become self-aware, identify your triggers. Know what pushes your buttons and what sets you off. You can't help when it happens, but you'll often see your kid's behaviors and emotions trigger certain behaviors and emotions in you. Often, those behaviors aren't even relevant to the situation. Separate your needs and feelings from the situation to allow you to respond appropriately.

Self-reflection can make you more aware of your thoughts, feelings, and behaviors. How do you self-reflect as a parent? You can start by asking yourself the following questions and writing your own answers:

- *Where do the ideas I have about parenting come from?*
- *What do I like about my parenting style?*
- *What don't I like about my parenting style?*
- *Where do my expectations about my kids come from?*
- *What would I like to change about my parenting style?*
- *What can I do to change my parenting approach as my child grows?*
- *What does my child need from me right now that is different from what I needed from my parents when I was a child?*

Your answers to these questions will help you discover more about yourself and how you're doing as a parent.

Are You a Good Parent?

What is your idea of being a good parent? Do you think being a good parent means you need to be around your kids 24/7? Do you think it means you need to buy tons of toys for your kid? Or that you must grant all your kid's requests?

I don't know what your definition of good parenting is, but I do hope you have one trait that your kids want from you. Overall, a good parent gives their child attention. A good parent is one that doesn't just buy gifts but is **present** with their child. Kids want you to notice them. They want you to make them feel loved and wanted. They want to see your eyes light up when they are around you. They don't want to feel like they're disturbing you all the time.

Are you familiar with other habits of a good parent? Different habits come together to make you a good parent. They are:

1. **Telling your child you love them**

What better way to let your kids know you love them than actually telling them? Don't assume your kids know how you feel about them without showing it in your actions and voicing it. Kids need to be assured, encouraged, and told that they are loved. It's always great to hear it from their parents. Make it a habit to always tell your kids you love them. Tell them how they make you feel.

Note that it is important you don't mistake love for material things. Many parents think they've fulfilled their role as parents by buying material things such as trendy clothes, toys, the latest game systems, bikes, etc. Of course, gift-giving can be a way of showing how much you care about your kids, but it isn't what they really *need*. Yes, from your kid's perspective, it can be sweet of you to give them these things, but it isn't the love they are ultimately seeking.

> In the end, Kids won't remember that fancy toy or game you bought for them, they will remember the time you Spent with them - Kevin Heath

Loving actions can include putting down your phone or other electronic devices to listen to your child when they need your attention. It can be wrapping your arms around your child when they are talking to you. It can also be keeping to your word when you say it. For example, if you tell your child you're going to be somewhere, ensure you don't no-show or arrive late. Be there on time and follow through with your promise. The same thing applies when you promise to get them something. Always try to fulfill your promises.

For divorced parents who don't have custody of their child, I understand that telling your kids you love them can be difficult. Still, I encourage you to do it whenever you have the opportunity. You don't need to see your kids physically to communicate. You can do that during phone calls, video calls, or through a quick text. The goal is to maintain a daily connection with your child by always letting them know how you truly feel about them.

2. **Staying involved in your child's life**

With so much to do every day, it's not surprising that our lives keep getting busier. In many families, both parents need to work 9 to 5.

They may have no help with chores such as cooking, washing the dishes, mopping, yard work, making the beds, and so on. There are just so many things to do that you'll hardly have time for yourself or your kid. It doesn't get easier for stay-at-home parents either. Again, there are so many things to do, and you'll likely not keep up half the time.

Amid all the chaos, don't forget that you need to be responsible for your child. Remember that your child is young, and they shouldn't be left on their own much. Please don't leave them to themselves. It's not just about showing up at school functions. Are you fully involved in their activities? While you need to be physically present with your child, you need to do more. You need to be involved in their lives and know what they're doing. Many parents feel their job is done when they simply buy Legos, cookies, or Play-doh for their kids. But your kids want you to play with Legos *together*, bake cookies *together*, and use Play-Doh *together* to make funny shapes.

It would be great if you could schedule fifteen to thirty minutes to spend with your child each day. Depending on what you think works best for your family, this time can be as short or as long as needed.

Please, no lecturing, scolding, or correction in these moments. Only try to have a good time with your kids. These priceless moments will make a huge difference in your life and your child's life. Your child will remember those moments you've set aside for them. Of course, we all know that time passes quickly. At this moment, your kids are seeking your attention, but in the blink of an eye, they'll turn a certain age when they won't need you anymore. So be involved now, when it's possible.

3. **Remaining consistent**

How consistent are you with your rules and boundaries? Does your **yes** mean **yes**? Does your **no** mean **no**? It's funny how we all know children need rules and boundaries, yet they always find a way to get past them. Your rules serve as the bedrock for your kids' values and actions; they rely on you to set healthy boundaries to make their world more understandable.

I have been guilty of letting boundaries slide. For example, there is a rule I set for my son that he can't use his iPad after 8 pm (his bedtime). However, when I was busy with something in the past, I tended to allow him to use his iPad a little longer just to keep him distracted. This way, I could focus on what I was doing. This back-and-forth expectation confused my son. He didn't know what was allowed and what wasn't because the time limit kept changing. I was inconsistent.

Inconsistencies like this example can encourage kids to test what they can or can't do. As you can imagine, this creates opportunities for power struggles. As a result, both of you get stressed and frustrated.

Ensure you stay consistent and follow through with your rules. Doing so enables your kids to predict how you'll react if they break the rules. They'll know you'll do as you say.

At the end of the day, remember that we aren't striving for perfection. We only want to do things that are humanly possible while offering our kids consistency. At the same time, we need to live by the same rules of behavior that we've set for our kids. Our children are always watching us and can call us out when we are inconsistent.

4. **Being respectful of your children**

Kids are still growing and have little experience in real-life situations. But when it comes to their opinions on certain matters, do you ignore their ideas because you think they're too young to have opinions? I made the mistake of not respecting my son's needs, and I hope you don't do the same.

Let me quickly share one of my awful stories with you here. I used to have a family friend whom I sometimes met up with and chatted with. My son expressed the fact he didn't care for my friend's daughter although they were the same age. Even though I knew my son didn't like her much, we still visited the family and invited them to our home many times. My son would cry and protest that he didn't want to go to their house or have them over, but I didn't care. I ignored my son's feelings and thought he was overreacting. I saw no reason for his displeasure.

Thinking about it now, I know that my son must have felt miserable and helpless at that time, and to make it worse, I didn't care. I should have acknowledged my son's emotions and respected them.

Your respect for your kids is evident when you listen to them without interrupting them, even when you know what they want to say. Allow your kids to make certain choices and decisions. Don't hesitate to let them know that you recognize they're making an effort with something. How you treat your child greatly impacts how they see themselves. So do better and be respectful of your little one. They will likely become a mom or dad later themselves, and you want to help them form better connections with their own children.

5. Remembering your actions speak louder than words

You've probably heard the popular saying, *"Don't just talk the talk, but also walk the walk."* This advice applies here because it's important to talk to your kids about your personal values, beliefs, and passions, but you should also demonstrate these parts of your life through your actions.

For example, let's say you just talked to your kids about how important respecting family members is. Just a moment later, you yell at them for something they did. There's a problem here: You aren't practicing what you preach. This inconsistency can confuse your kids and make them lose respect for you. Let your actions speak just as loudly as your voice. Ensure your values, beliefs, and passions are reflected by your actions.

Poor parenting skills?

"Am I a bad parent?"

This is a question you've probably asked yourself after you've had a rough day with your child. It's easy to feel overwhelmed and doubt your parenting skills when having one of these moments. Likewise, you'll feel your parenting skills are below par when you're feeling exhausted, lost, and impatient with nothing going your way.

Sometimes, it feels like all your choices have monumental consequences and that you are always making the *wrong* choice. You worry about the long-term effects these decisions can have on your relationship with your child. But don't forget that we all make mistakes, and learning from your mistakes makes us better parents.

Have you ever taken the time to wonder what qualities make someone a bad parent? It's important to note that the concept of a "bad parent" is subjective and can vary depending on cultural, social, and individual factors. However, some common categories of bad parenting behaviors include:

1. **They never guide**

Of course, we know that one of the most crucial aspects of parenting is giving the proper guidance to our kids while they're young and gaining experience. However, bad parents are ones who never guide. They are usually busy with their own priorities and have no time to spare to guide their kids on important decisions. Bad parents want their kids to do only what they ask and won't listen to what the kids want.Since they're usually in a bad mood, their kids will avoid coming to them. This distance may create bigger problems later.

2. **They are overly concerned**

Don't get me wrong. I'm not suggesting that being concerned about your child isn't good. However, when you overdo it by being overprotective and prying into every detail of your child's life, it can be annoying and cause a disconnect. Even though they're just kids, they need their space as well. They need time to solve minor issues independently, and being overly concerned will deprive your kids of learning.

3. **They are helicopter parents**

Helicopter parents are bossy and want things to always go their way, regardless of how it makes their kids feel. They pressure their kids to do the parent's bidding. When the kids object, they act like military officers, giving orders and punishments. Helicopter parents are excessively strict over everything and never loosen up with their kids.

4. **They have high expectations**

We all have set goals and dreams of how we want our kids to be. However, while we hope for the best, some things may not go as planned. When this is the case, we don't need to beat ourselves up over it. For example, while you've dreamt of your son becoming a doctor, he might develop an interest in something else and choose a different career path.

Not every child is the same. Therefore, parents need to be reasonable with their expectations and be patient with their child's unique growth process.

5. **They are abusive**

Abusive parenting refers to a pattern of behavior by a parent or caregiver that harms a child physically, emotionally, or psychologically. It can cause a serious problem that can have lasting effects on a child's well-being. Below can be considered abusive parenting:

Physical abuse: This involves the use of physical force that causes injury, such as hitting, kicking, or shaking a child.

Emotional abuse: This involves behaviors that damage a child's self-esteem, such as constant criticism, belittling, or name-calling. It can also involve threats of harm or abandonment.

Sexual abuse: Any sexual activity between an adult and a child, including touching, penetration, or exposure.

Psychological abuse: This can harm a child's mental and emotional well-being, such as withholding affection, isolating the child from others, or threatening child.

6. **They like comparing their children to others**

As I mentioned, not every child is the same, not even twins. Comparing your kid to others can make your child feel bad about themselves. It can affect their self-confidence and even make them depressed.

If the kid is being compared negatively to his siblings, cousins, friends, or neighbors, he will eventually feel that something about him is unacceptable to you. Comparisons make kids feel hurt, and your child will try to maintain distance from you. Don't compare your child to others. There's no comparison between the sun and the moon. They shine when it's their time. Remember, you can't be a perfect mother or father, just as your child can't be a perfect kid.

Please note that therapy can be beneficial for parents or children who have experienced trauma or who are struggling with emotional or behavioral issues. There are many resources available, such as online communities, parenting classes, counseling, and support groups. So, do not hesitate to reach out and seek support when you need it.

Finally, let me ask again: Who are you? Do you feel like you're a good parent? I believe the five aspects of good parenting I've discussed in this chapter will give you some insight into who you are.

> Anyone can have a child and call themselves " a parent"
> A real parent is someone who puts that child above their own selfish needs and wants.

Please Review My Book
You Can Make A Difference

I hope you're enjoying the book and ask if you can spare a quick moment to write a review or hit the star rating to help me keep going. I appreciate your help.

Chapter 9

Time to Connect with Your Kids

"We're all imperfect parents & that's perfectly ok. Tiny humans need connection not perfection." – L.R. Knost

Before we became parents, we longed for bonding moments with our kids. We envisioned the perfect life we'd have with our *"mini-me."* But now that we're parents, we're so caught up in the hassle of life that we begin to lose touch with one of the most important things in our lives – our kids.

With so many activities like work, childcare, chores, and school, we parents don't have much time left to spend with our kids. Today, parents are busy with their work and personal lives and have little or no extended family support. This means they spend less time with their kids than ever before. Even when they have a few moments to spend with their kids, parents still get distracted by computers, phones, and TV. They attempt to cope with the stress by doing too many things simultaneously.

Time passes quickly, and if we keep going about our lives in this way, we may lose out on our kid's childhood completely. It's ironic because that's exactly the thing we've looked forward to for so long. Remember that kids are biologically wired to seek secure attachment. When they don't have it, all hell lets loose. Yet when their need for connection is met, they become more patient with you and listen better.

Kids function at their best when they feel connected to you. This connection helps guide them. They will be more easygoing and eager to act appropriately. Throughout this chapter, we will focus on connection as the secret ingredient that makes parenting easier, not to mention more joyful. If you want more sweetness from your child, then connection is the way to get it.

Filling the Love Cup

You may wonder what a love cup is and how it relates to connecting with your kids. Well, stay with me. You'll learn about the whole idea behind the notion of "filling the love cup" soon.

First, let's imagine that two people (a man and his neighbor) are planting acorns in the hopes of growing huge oak trees. The man tends to the acorn and nurtures it until it becomes an oak sapling. Then, the man leaves the sapling alone, hoping everything turns out well. He starts to neglect it. After a few years of not giving the tree the attention it deserves, it became less attractive. The leaves and trunk became too thin.

On the other hand, the neighbor, who also plants an acorn, makes sure he keeps watering the sapling daily. He nurtures the plant with love and attention. After a few years, the tree becomes very beautiful and full of healthy leaves and stems. The trunk is very sturdy and provides shade for people.

Imagine that the trees are humans for a minute. I know that sounds crazy, but bear with me. Those acorns need you to nurture them with good soil, adequate water, and the right weather conditions. In other words, they need you to fill their cups with love to survive and grow. Kids need you to do the same for them.

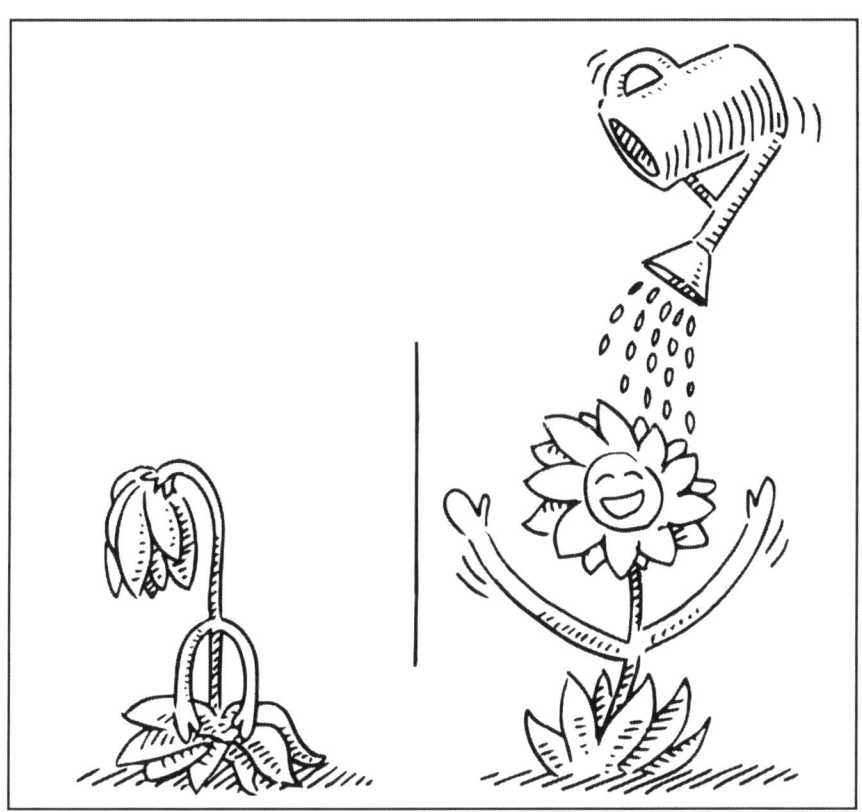

Despite your busy schedule, you must treat your kids lovingly. Doing so will help them believe they are loved. When kids aren't treated as the valuable individuals they are, they will likely believe something is wrong with them. Can we really blame them?

Think about when you were younger. How would you have felt if your parents constantly yelled at you and never acknowledged anything good that you did? You would likely come to believe that you were the problem. You probably wouldn't stop to think that something is wrong with how you're being treated.

If parents keep talking down to their kids instead of filling them with love, the kids will think they mean nothing to anyone. Self-doubt will creep in. How kids are treated determines whether they have healthy or unhealthy self-esteem later in life.

What Fills a Child's Love Cup?

To understand what and how to fill your child's love cup, let's first discuss what drains the cup in the first place.

Here are things that may trigger emptying your child's love cup:

- Constant yelling and scolding
- Giving harsh punishments
- Isolation and loneliness
- Negative words
- Forcing kids to do what they hate
- Parents fighting
- Unstable home environment
- Non-affectionate parents
- Hatred or rejection

This is a list of the negative interactions that can dry up your child's love quickly. Consider which of your actions might be emptying your child's love cup even though you haven't been aware of it.

Now, let's discuss what *fills* a child's love cup. The three main ingredients are unconditional love, play, and quality time.

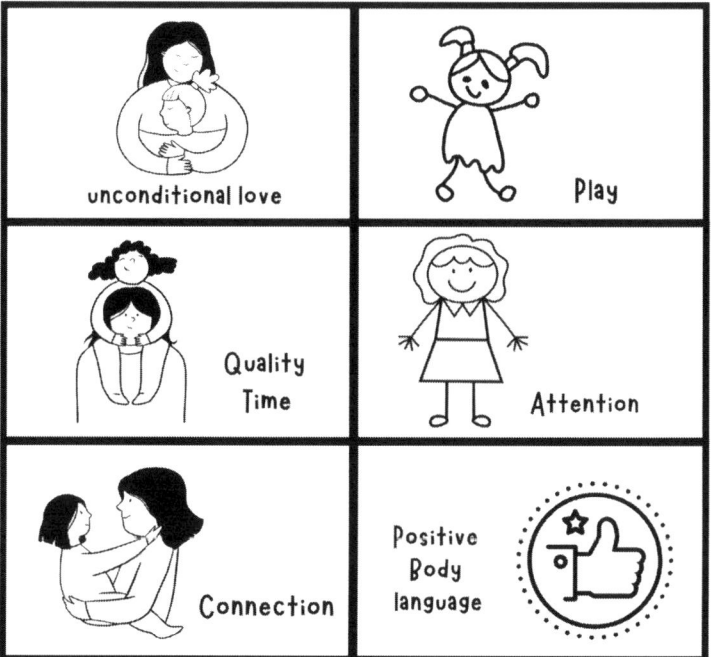

Unconditional Love

What does unconditional love mean to you?

Many people think they understand what unconditional love means even though they don't. In simple terms, unconditional love is love without strings attached. It means your love for your kids isn't based on what they can give you, nor is it dependent on whom they become or their actions toward you.

When your kids drive you crazy, how do you feel about them? Do you still love them unconditionally? Of course, you should, even if it's difficult. Think of unconditional love as a muscle that needs a daily workout. You need to train your brain to:

- Accept that your child is an immature human that makes mistakes and will learn from them as they keep growing and improving.
- Accept your child for whom they are without comparing them to others. Know that your child is enough just the way they are.

Another pressure that tests parents' love for their kids is when they want their kids to become successful and do great things. As a result, they push their kids to achieve more than they can, sometimes even before elementary school starts. We know that parents do this out of love and that they have the best intention for their kids. They simply want to see their kids do great things. But pushing them beyond their limits does more harm than good.

Kids don't need to pass your standards before receiving your love. High expectations from you can weaken the bond between you and your child. Regardless of what happens or what your children do, ensure that the love you show your kids is constant. Always love your children for who they are and treat them as priceless gifts.

Play

Play is another way to connect with your child and fill their emotional cup. Can you remember all the silly faces you made to make your kids laugh when they were babies? Perhaps you dressed like a clown, danced without music, or sang a ridiculous tune to get their attention and stop their tears. Oh, how beautiful life was then! But now that your kids have grown older and can play on their own, playtime with them is very minimal (if there is any at all).

Don't forget that play is the language of kids, and you shouldn't stop doing it with them. There aren't many limitations to the activities you can engage in with your kids. Do what you both enjoy! Some fun ideas include playing roughhouse, chase, or hide and seek. The laughs that come from playing fill your kid's emotional cup and leave less room for unwanted behaviors.

Quality Time

What if you spend the whole day with your kids yet don't feel connected to them? This isn't surprising because many parents have reported that they don't feel connected to their kids in the same way that they used to. Why is this a problem? Furthermore, how can you spend twenty-four hours at home and not feel a connection to your kid?

Undeniably, kids need attention. But have you been giving your kids attention, thinking you'll feel connected just by doing that? If so, you might have been confusing attention with connection. The truth is, you can pay attention to your kids and still feel no emotional connection. Instead, what kids need is high-quality time and engagement with you.

Many parents believe they spend quality time with their kids by taking them to their favorite spots like parks, stores, and other places. However, the quality of the time spent together is determined by *how* you spend time with your kids while at these locations. When you're with them, do you take a break from your devices and stay focused on your kids? Are you thinking about the work emails you must respond to or the project report you need to submit? Are you mindfully present, not allowing your mind to wander?

How long you spend time with your kids isn't all that matters. What really matters is how well you do it. Ensure you play games you both can do because the more you engage in an activity with them, the more connected you will feel with them. Get rid of distractions and give your kids your full attention. Remember, they don't need twenty-four hours of attention from you. Even a few minutes of quality time makes a huge difference.

Your Body Language

Nonverbal communication plays an important role when we pass information to our kids. It says a lot about our feelings and the people around us. Regardless of their ages, children pick up our nonverbal cues in powerful ways. They notice when we laugh, smile, cry, wink, or frown.

Just as we can read our kids' expressions, children can pick up and understand how we feel through these expressions even when we don't open our mouths. They do this by reading our body language.

Let's imagine that your child is holding a bottle of milk and spills it. As you run into the kitchen to see what happened, you find the entire floor is covered in milk. What do you do? You've learned that yelling isn't a good way to parent, so you're holding back your anger inside. However, you can't hide your nonverbal expressions such as your facial expression or tone of voice. Even when you aren't yelling, your body language shows anger and disappointment. So, what's the difference then?

Do not worry that Children never listen to you; worry that they are always watching you.

- Robert Fulghum

As a parent, you should be conscious of the nonverbal cues you give when you're around your kids because they influence how your kids perceive and respond to you. For example, if you are constantly on edge, acting frustrated, or nagging, there's a high chance your child might pick up on these behaviors and respond negatively.

Think back to your childhood. You would probably agree with me that you learned many habits from your parents and the other people around you. The same goes for your kids. They mirror your behavior and learn from you. You're already helping develop your child's nonverbal communication skills.

Three Ways to Adjust Your Body Language

Luckily, there are methods you can use to improve your nonverbal communication skills and quickly adjust your body language. You can make sure your expressions speak love to your little ones, no matter their age.

Note that as you practice your own good nonverbal communication skills, you're teaching your kids how to improve their own communication skills.

- **Face your children**

Do you face your kids when you talk to them most of the time? Sometimes, we neglect this simple but essential aspect of communication. We often talk to our kids while we're busy focusing on something else. Even when we don't mean to divide our attention, not facing our kids when talking to them has become normal for many parents.

I remember always talking to my son while I was doing the dishes, mopping the floor, doing the laundry, or cooking. I was constantly distracted and rarely gave him my full attention. When parents repeatedly speak to their kids while distracted, detachment is inevitable. What if you had something important to tell your partner, and they watched TV instead of listening to you and giving you their full attention? How would you feel? Annoyed, right? You'd probably feel ignored and disconnected from them.

It's the same for kids. If you're engrossed with a different task while they're talking to you, and they have to raise their voice to get your attention, how do you think they are going to feel? Similarly, if your kid has to chase after you to get a response, or they're always talking to your back, they're going to feel distanced from you.

You need to warm up to your kids. Face them when you're talking to them. Let them see your face and your expressions as you're listening. Take a break from whatever you're working on and give your kids a few minutes to talk. Have a proper conversation. Your kids deserve your respect and attention.

- **Use enough physical contact**

Children respond well to physical contact (touch), especially from their parents. This nonverbal communication directly conveys your emotions and feelings to your little ones.

Gentle hugs and kisses are ways to send a million silent words to your kids without opening your mouth. They will immediately feel warm, safe, and loved without you needing to say much. How? Because your kids can feel your body language from the moment you make contact with them.

Caught up in a fast-paced world, we sometimes forget how important these little actions are. Therefore, try to include physical contact when you interact with your kids. You can gently wrap your arms around them when they're sad or upset. A light kiss shows you love and appreciate them. A small gesture like this could be all they need to feel reassured and keep you connected.

Here are some other ways you can connect through physical contact with your children:

- Hold hands when walking
- Sit close when you read a book together
- Cuddle them before bed
- Have a special handshake
- Rub their back while you are talking to them
- Lightly tickle them

Physical contact with your kid assures them that you're present and in the moment with them. You're using your actions to tell them they have your undivided attention.

- **Make eye contact**

According to a popular saying, *"The eyes are the windows to the soul."* And I agree. When you interact with your kids and maintain a certain level of eye contact, you're connecting on a deeper level with them. They'll feel like they've got your attention, and they'll give you their attention in return. Your child will instantly feel drawn to the conversation because they know you're showing them that you value and respect what they're saying.

Remember that kids will mirror what they see their parents doing. You're teaching them communication skills by showing them the importance of eye contact.

Research has shown that eye contact with your kid can sync your brain waves with theirs. This can improve communication, attachment, and bonding between you two, increasing their sense of security. Eye contact also allows your kid's brain to develop and stay on track. The more connected you are to your baby, the more you encourage their emotional development.

Making these three quick changes to your nonverbal communication shows your kids that you value them through your actions. Furthermore, you're developing their nonverbal communication skills to help them learn and understand their emotions and other people's.

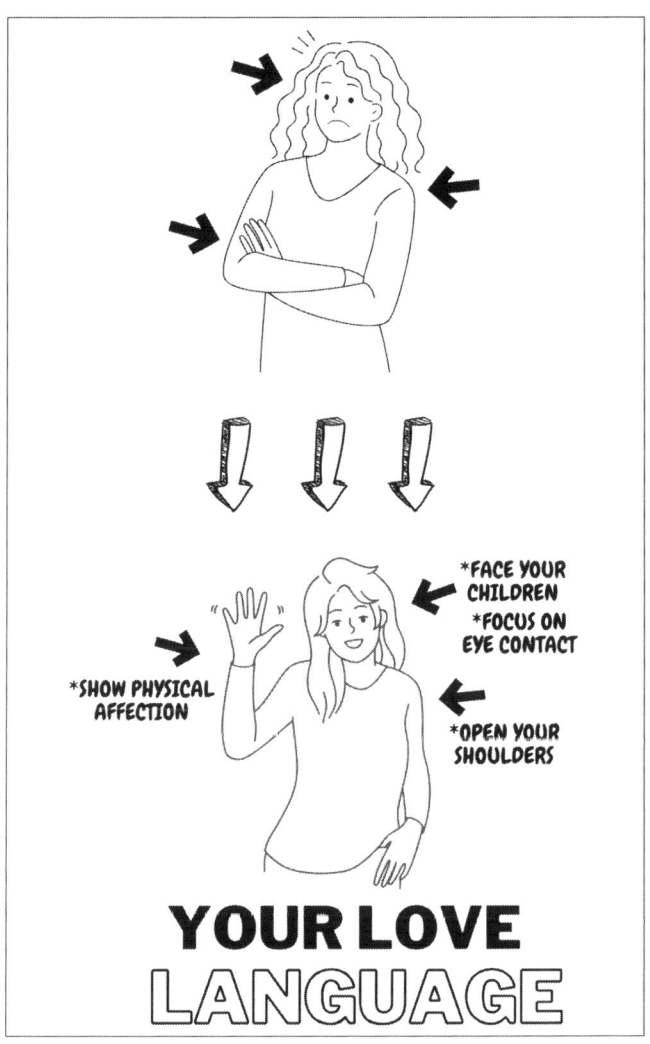

Chapter 10

Connection Before Correction

"You have to reach the heart before you can teach the head."
- Dr. Jane Nelsen

P icture this. You've just bought some delicious treats from the bakery on the way home after a long day at work. You sit down on the sofa and started eating it. You are so happy until you hear your partner say mockingly, *"Look at your belly. Are you eight months pregnant? You never stop eating! That's why you're not losing weight."* You know you're thirty pounds overweight, which already makes you feel very depressed.

How would you feel facing such criticism from your partner as they shame your body instead of giving you a warm welcome? I'm certain your partner's remark would hurt and make you feel worse than you already do.

You can imagine the pain, the embarrassment, and the intense anger you would feel.

You might wonder, *"How can someone who is supposed to be my support system be so heartless? He thinks I'm fat and ugly. Does he even love me?"* These are some of the questions you'll likely ask yourself as you feel a distance growing between you two.

You know he is worried about your weight gain and how it affects your health, but how he approached the situation was bad. He could have started, *"Honey, you must be so tired and hungry eating like that. Why don't you have an apple before dinner?"* This approach would make you feel warm and loved.

But did you know that kids experience similar feelings? They also deal with big emotions when they're met with your many commands.

"Don't do that!"

"Stop it!"

"Get out of here!"

While discovering their special place in the world, kids act in ways that are far from adorable. They push limits, explore, experiment, and show off their independence. As parents, watching them do these things can bring us to our knees, and we might start yelling and saying things we regret. Well, we're only human, and our emotions can override us.

Instead of jumping right into correcting your kids and yelling at them, why not try connecting with them first? It's just like charging a dead phone before using it. We need to connect to our children first. Connection may be what's preventing you from enjoying your parenting experience. Let's find out how to connect.

We want to connect

When their kids misbehave, parents are quick to ask, *"What should I do?"* It's easy for parents to turn to relatives, friends, books, blogs, and support groups to find effective ways to stop their kid's difficult behaviors. They want to fix the situation immediately. But parents fail to understand that there are few quick fixes when it comes to parenting. The tools are secondary to the relationship they have with their kids. Parents should focus on how to connect first.

Parenting involves building a relationship with your child. It's not just about using a set of strategies. You need to have a relationship with your kids first in order to use the strategies, and you'll need to parent from the heart.

How to Connect with Your Child

When your kids feel connected to you, they will feel loved, understood, and valued. As a result, they will be more open to your influence. Put yourself in their shoes. Don't you feel open to your partner's influence when they make you feel loved, respected, listened to, and understood?

You know the amazing benefits of connecting with your kids and want to do it. Still, you keep wondering, *"How can I find the time for connection when I barely even have time for myself? I need to work, check their homework, cook, clean, and do so many things in just twenty-four hours. How can I find time to connect with my kids?"*

The truth is, you don't need the whole day to connect with your kids. As I mentioned in the last chapter, it is all about quality time, not *quantity*. Aim to make the time you spend with them worthwhile, even if it's just a few minutes. On that note, here are four ways you can be more intentional about bonding and connecting with your kids.

1. **Unplug from electronics**

Can you really blame kids for spending so much time watching TV and using other devices when you're guilty of the same thing? Despite our busy schedules, we always find a way to squeeze out time to chat, be on social media, and watch YouTube videos or Netflix!

Why do we complain that we have too little time when we make time for all these timewasters? We don't always have our priorities right. Of course, we are humans and need to connect with friends and know what's going on with them. But we need to set aside time with our kids. And when we are with them, they deserve our undivided attention. So, try and unplug from electronic devices and don't allow them to serve as distractions.

Take a break from the computer screen, put down your phone, and give your child that undivided attention. Kids are smart and know when you are focused on them. Once they notice this, it's easier for them to feel loved, heard, and supported. They will warm up to you quickly.

2. **Listen without offering advice**

As adults, it's easy to cut your kids off and prevent them from explaining further because you think you know better. After all, you've been in their shoes and know better (so you think). I understand your intentions. You want to help, and you don't want to prolong the issue. But kids love to be heard. When they see that you aren't interested in listening to them, they'd rather keep to themselves.

Our kids need to know that we are there for them, we empathize with them, and we want the best for them. Listen to them. Allow them to explain, rant, and otherwise offload their feelings without cutting them off or giving advice. You still have plenty of time to give advice later, so save it until your kid's done talking. I know it isn't always easy to be patient with them but know that when they are at their worst, they need you the most.

3. **Show interest in what they love**

The latest update of Candy Crush is out, but of course, you're probably not as excited as your kids. Meanwhile, one way to show your kids they're important to you is to show some genuine interest in them.

You can't always be an adult when it comes to parenting. You have to bring out that inner child to connect with them on the same frequency.

Imagine that you like sewing. One day, you're excited to show off the new patterns you sewed on your bed cover with your new embroidery machine. But your husband doesn't understand why you spend the whole day sewing these *ugly* patterns on your blankets. He even thinks your hobby should be reserved for grandmas. He shows no interest or appreciation for your craft or effort. How would you feel?

The moment you see your husband's disinterested face, you feel disconnected from him and don't want to talk to him. Not only does he not care for the things you like, but he also thinks your embroideries are ugly. Of course, you're going to feel he doesn't care about you, right? You expect he should at least show a little interest. He could take time to appreciate your time and effort with a small compliment like, *"Wow, your designs are beautiful,"* or *"You did great, honey! Keep it up."*

If you can feel this way as an adult, then you can imagine how sad and disconnected kids feel when you don't show interest in what they like. Have your kids ever complained saying, *"You never understand me!," "Forget it!," or "You never get it!"?* If any of these statements don't sound familiar, then you must be doing well with your kids! It's easy for your kids to become disconnected from you when you show no interest in what they do.

You don't need to like their hobby as they do. Just showing that you're interested is enough to make them feel loved. Don't give them that disapproving look or shake your head. Instead, give them a smile and say something encouraging. For example, you can say, *"Oh great! This looks like so much fun!"* Remember that they're kids, and their interests will keep changing with age.

When you share your kids' passions, you're not just telling them you care about them; you're showing them you support them. This will help them know how important they are in your life because you're dedicating your valuable time to be with them.

Why Connection Before Correction

The idea of connection before correction is that children only learn from people they trust and feel connected to. Children are more willing to learn when they're in an ongoing relationship that has friendship, mutual respect, and attention at the foundation.

Connection-based parenting, in essence, means that every time you interact with your child, you focus on connecting first, which means you open your child's heart first. You connect before playing, connect before communicating, and connect before correcting or disciplining.

If you're familiar with Aesop's fables, you might know the story about the North Wind and the Sun. The North Wind tried to blow the coat off, but the man just held onto it tighter. Then, the Sun warmed on the man, and he became so hot that he willingly took off his coat.

Like the story's takeaway point, force and violence can't open your child's heart. Still, by connecting and sharing your kid's feelings, you'll be able to easily get through to them.

As a young mom, I first came across the concept of connection before correction when my son was little. The first thought that came to my head was, *"What kind of connection is stronger than the mother and son bond we already share? Absolutely nothing!"* Of course, I'm the mother. What other connection are they talking about? And why would I ever want to correct this sweet little human? What could he do wrong?

Little did I know that I was just starting out with gentle parenting, and there was a whole new world I never knew existed. Now that I know, I'm glad to share my thoughts with you.

Why Connection First is Important in Parenting

Connection is important in parenting because:

- **It encourages positive communication.** When you connect before correcting, you are paving the way for better communication between you and your child in a supportive and positive way. This can create more openness and honesty between you, building a strong parent-child relationship.
- **It helps build trust.** When you're emotionally connected with your child, they are more likely to trust and rely on you, making it easier for you to guide them and correct their behaviors when necessary.
- **It encourages cooperation.** When your child feels supported and connected to you, they will likely cooperate with you and in turn, you can help shape their behaviors.
- **It helps with emotional regulation.** When your child feels connected to you, they will likely feel secure and safe with you. This feeling helps regulate their emotions and act more appropriately.

Connection Before Correction

What should you do when your child does something wrong? Normal, knee-jerk reactions are scolding, yelling, or handing out punishments, but connection before correction says you should *connect* first.

Here's an example. Let's say you are at the park with your child who sees a toy they want. They grab it from another kid without asking. Normally, we would scold them and say, *"No, you don't do that."* We might also frown at them so they know such actions are unacceptable.

Doing that means you skipped the connection part and went straight to correcting. Connection before correction says you connect first by showing some positive intent. For example, you could say, *"Hey J! I see you like that toy and want to play with it. I also think it's pretty cool."*

Next, you can give your kid an assuring hug to deepen the connection and tell them, *"If you want to play with someone else's toy, you need to ask them instead of taking it."* This way, you don't get upset and just focus on what your child did wrong. Instead, you show them you're dependable to guide and help them. This way, they can feel the connection between the two of you.

Like Alfred Adler and Rudolf Dreikurs said, kids will develop "a sense of belonging and significance." Moreover, children thrive, grow, feel safe, and learn best when they feel a connection in your ongoing relationship.

Experts suggest that children cannot be positively influenced until we create a connection with them. We need to stop focusing on what our kids do wrong. Instead, we should mend our relationships and connect with them to make them feel secure, wanted, loved, cared for, and noticed. I've always viewed the concept of connection before correction as a **brain** and **heart** thing.

In the previous chapter, we talked about filling the love cup. Every child needs someone who makes them feel special, loves them unconditionally, and fills their love cup. This love cup is a metaphor for a container of their positive emotions. One of the best ways to build connections with kids is to be that person who acknowledges their emotional needs and knows how to fill their love cup.

Spending time filling a child's love cup is the easiest way to connect with your child and get a high score on proactive parenting.

Building a connection with our kids will help us improve our relationships, but giving in to every demand a child makes is not an effective parenting method. Fortunately, we can instead use a method of positive discipline that shows the child we still care.

Take this example of a child who wants chocolate.

Child: Mom, I want another piece of chocolate!

Mom: You had enough today.

Child: But I want more, please, Mom. Just one more!

Mom: You know I love you and would give you more if you could have it. But I have to say, "No" this time.

Having a bar of chocolate is okay but wanting three or four more could be bad for their teeth. The mom knows this and assures her child of her love first before politely refusing to give in to her child's demands.

When you yell or criticize children for misbehaving at every opportunity, there's a possibility that your child will pull back from you. They might close off their emotions from you. Remember that force and violence won't foster learning, but positive connections can encourage kids to change and learn.

When children feel connected, they'll feel they can trust you and listen to you. These are the teachable moments when you can make a significant impact. These moments are when they're willing to listen and learn.

As you learn about the many positive discipline tools available, remember that they are mostly designed to create a connection. You still need to offer respectful correction.

It is important to understand that correction, as practiced in positive discipline, differs significantly from traditional correction. These are two worlds apart because traditional correction revolves around punishment. Traditional correction focuses on grounding, scolding, taking away privileges, yelling, blaming, and punitive time-outs to name a few common forms of correction. Consequently, traditional discipline mostly involves adults doing something or imposing their authority on kids. On the other hand, correction in positive discipline involves kids. This type of correction focuses on finding solutions together whenever possible. Through positive discipline, you can connect with your kids to teach them how things are supposed to be done instead of putting them down emotionally.

I end this chapter with a popular quote that hits home: *"When you keep criticizing your kids, they don't stop loving you. They stop loving themselves."* Finally, remember to model the behavior you want your kids to emulate.

When you keep criticizing your kids, they don't stop loving you. They stop loving themselves.

Part Five

Connected Family

We argue, we fight. We even stop talking to each other at times. But in the end, family is family…
The love & connection will always be there.

Chapter 11

Become a Better Parent

"Your children will become who you are; so be who you want them to be."- Anonymous

I want you to grab a sheet of paper and a pen and take a few moments to think about the kind of parent you want to be. How would you like your child to view you after they grow up? What kind of stories do you want them to tell their kids about you, their grandparents?

Of course, we all wish we were better parents. We all wish we had the right responses to the parenting problems we face. We want to have the answers to all our children's questions. But we should never forget that we're imperfect humans. While making mistakes is unavoidable, it's important to learn from them and always strive to be good parents.

Being a good parent isn't a walk in the park. It can be difficult, especially since no instruction manual comes with your baby when you give birth. Many of us have to learn on the job. This is a sad reality.

However, if you want to improve your parenting skills by becoming a better parent and connecting with your child more, this chapter can help you. Here, we discuss parenting tips that strengthen the bond with your child regardless of their needs and age. We'll focus on making one of the hardest jobs on earth easier!

Are You a Good Role Model?

Do you think you're a good role model for your kids? Being a good role model is an important characteristic your kids need you to demonstrate. Even though there are so many other role model options they can choose from, ranging from teachers, peers, cartoon characters, and athletes, they look to their parent as their number one role model. Think about it. Your child is more likely to mimic what you do. For example, when you repeatedly sing a favorite song at home, you will notice that your child begins to sing that song over time.

You shouldn't be surprised because kids imitate everything we do. Kids learn everything they know through imitation: how to speak, clap, dance, sing, and dress up. Therefore, they focus on what you *do* more than what you *say*. Since you know that kids will see what you model and imitate those actions, whether positive or negative, parents need to be good role models.

You can either be an important protective factor (environmental influence) that protects your kids against problematic behaviors, or you can be a powerful risk factor (environmental condition) linked with increasing problematic behavior in kids.

Before we discuss how you can be a *good* role model for your kids, let's quickly look at what it means to be a good role model.

What is a Good Role Model?

While we all have different definitions of what or who a good role model is, most people agree on the following:

- **A good role model has passion and the ability to inspire others.** As parents, you should be dedicated to helping and empowering your child in all aspects of their lives.
- **A good role model has a clear set of values.** Kids love people who support their beliefs because it makes them aware that their values define who they are.
- **A good role model is selfless and accepting of others.** Kids love people who accept them as they are, without comparing them with other kids.
- **A good role model has the ability to overcome obstacles.** Who wouldn't want a knight in shining armor to be there to help? It's always great when kids know they can run to their parents with any problem because they know good parents always have a solution.

Let's elaborate on what a good role model for kids is. David Streight, the executive director of the Council for Spiritual and Ethical Education and a nationally certified school psychologist, says this about role models:

- The right modeling can influence the amount of empathy your child feels and shows later in life.
- Your actions and how you model for your kids influence your child to grow up with good consciences and with well-developed moral reasoning skills.
- Kids with good role models are more generous. They are more inclined to act for the benefit of others without expecting anything in return.
- With a good role model, kids understand how to act in difficult situations they may likely face in life.

One of the most powerful tools in parenting, a good role model skillset can be used to your advantage. You can pass on values to your kids, and they will become the kind of adults you want them to be.

How to Be an Effective Role Model for Your Children

Before we discuss how to be an effective role model for your children, let me quickly introduce you to a fable that sheds light on how role modeling works.

The following conversation is between two crabs, a mother and child. The crabs are leaving their home and taking a stroll on the sand.

Mother crab: *"Hey, why are you walking so clumsily? Why not walk in a straight line?"*

Baby crab: *"But Mom! I am walking the same way you do."*

Mother crab: *"No, you're not. Now, look carefully at how I walk."*

Baby crab: *"Then you need a mirror, Mom. I am following the example you set."*

So, what did you learn from this fable? You are what your child is. If you want your child to be kind, you need to be kind. If you want them to be respectful, then be respectful to your child. If you don't want your child to hit others, don't hit your child.

For most parents, being an effective role model for their kids will require much self-control, hard work, and forethought. Remember, your kids are always watching you. They're examining your attitudes, actions, and beliefs. These ideas will get integrated into your child's being, so it's essential that you're intentional about what traits you model for your children.

Now that you're aware of this huge responsibility you have on your shoulders, you can be encouraged to get better. If you want to make it less likely for your child to gravitate toward alcohol later in the future, you should get rid of those bottles and stay away from alcohol yourself. The same thing applies to smoking. You should quit smoking if you don't want your child to emulate you. The reason for this is simple. Kids will feel comfortable doing certain things if they've seen them done at home. So don't get caught up in your emotions and show too much anger. You don't know if you are creating a small "volcano" that is just as angry as you.

The following are strategies you can use to become an effective role model.

- *Walk the Talk*

For most parents, the quote *"Do as I say, not as I do"* simply doesn't work for them. Kids are like the best detectives and can sniff out insincerity, hypocrisy, and deceit like a bloodhound. They tend to believe and look up to parents that have shown consistency in their actions and words. But, unfortunately, it's not just about *showing* them. It's about "walking the talk."

If you're a parent that doesn't want their kids to lie and feign sickness to avoid doing chores, you shouldn't lie about being sick to get out of work. On the other hand, if you want your child to reduce their screen time, then be a good role model by limiting your device usage as well.

Just as you respect people who live by their rules, kids do the same. They respect adults who follow what they preach. When they sense hypocrisy in you, it immediately sends them looking for alternative role models.

- *Model Through Your Words*

Your kids don't just look for clues in your actions. They also listen to you more than you can imagine. How you speak, what you talk about, and which opinions you voice can influence your kid's values.

How do you speak to your child? What about your partner – how do you speak to them? And your friends, colleagues, and neighbors? What about the delivery person, the waitstaff at your favorite restaurant, and the cashier at the grocery store? If you're used to cursing and yelling at customer service staff over the phone, don't you think your child will pick up the same mannerisms from you? I hope not, but your kids may take it for granted that treating others this way is okay.

Ensure you model respect for others through your choice of words and tone of voice. The kind of words you use with people should show respect for the differences you have between the two of you.

Don't bully or threaten your kids with your words when they misbehave. Instead, respond with a discipline that's based on respect for your child. Know that they are human and bound to make mistakes. As kids, they are still learning and probably haven't learned how to be considerate, loving, and empathetic. It's left for you as their role model to demonstrate those behaviors.

Isn't it better to show that you follow your own advice rather than just say, "Be kind."? If you must, help your partner around the house and show your child what teamwork means. Teach them that picking up garbage to recycle and compost means they care about their world. Teach them that kindness can open the door for good things to come into their life.

Parenting Mindset

How you view and treat your child in difficult times matters a lot. These crucial points are important for establishing your parent-child relationship and the connection you and your kid share. Over the years of my intentional parenting journey, I've discovered that parenting life is only as hard as you think it is.

Think of parents who are raising children with disabilities. Many parents struggle with accepting the reality that their child has a disability. They might refuse to accept that they need to care for their child throughout their life. These parents might also worry about helping the child manage and adjust to their new reality.

I remember seeing a TV show where highly talented people performed on stage while judges scrutinized their performances and selected the best. What drew my attention was when a child with autism came on stage. His mother led him onto the stage because he was also blind.

The most intriguing part to me was that the mother never gave up on her child. She was able to identify his talent and develop it to the point that he could perform on one of the biggest stages in the world, wowing the judges and the entire audience. I was in tears when I saw the standing ovation he got.

The point here is that some parents see their child's disability as a stroke of bad luck. In contrast, some parents see it as a challenge that needs their attention. In other words, they rise to the occasion. Depending on your mindset, the choices and parenting approach you decide to take will either make or break your child.

Let's assume you get a call from school and learn that your child got into a fight for the second time that month. How would you react? Would you react harshly and treat your child as a troubled kid who *likes* getting into trouble? Or would you take a different approach by teaching your child how to be a better person by communicating and respecting others instead of fighting?

This example shows us two different ways to respond to a negative situation as a parent. As parents, we should fully understand how our mindsets affect and mold our kids. This is especially important because there's a thin line between a negative and a positive mindset.

So, what type of parenting mindset do you have? To determine this, you must first evaluate yourself and adjust your mindset accordingly because your children are your treasure.

Let's also look at two different ways parents can view their kids.

When you label your child as DIFFICULT and STUBBORN,

- You think your kid is the most difficult to get through to.
- You discuss your child's "stubbornness" with other people when the child is present.
- You've created an image of your child, and whether you're aware or not, you've already formed the mindset that your child is difficult and stubborn.
- This mindset will influence how you treat, respond to, and view your child.
- Over time, you'll label your child as DIFFICULT and STUBBORN. Your child will also begin to accept and view themselves as such.

When you consider your child's behavior to be an opportunity for empathy,

- You empathize with your child even when they're showing aggression or are in the middle of an outburst. This is so because they could be trying to reach out to you by acting out from feeling sad, scared, lonely, or in pain.
- You respect your child instead of belittling them or talking negatively about them to others when they are present.
- You choose to act or respond after you understand the reason behind your child's behavior, instead of concluding that they're just acting out and being difficult.

As a parent, when you objectively look at the core of your child's behavior, you may be less inclined to assign a negative label to your child.

I know this for a fact because I have personally experienced it. Before I started practicing gentle and intentional parenting, I used to see my son as a difficult child. I labeled him a **stubborn kid**, and I always found it challenging to get through to him. However, I never knew I was missing out on all the great things about my little treasure because I chose to focus only on the negatives.

I realized that I had been unfair with my labels. I wasn't seeing all the good in my son because of my mindset. Furthermore, I failed to identify and understand the things going on in his little world. I could not empathize or connect to his emotions, nor could I respond with compassion and give him the attention he needed.

When you can empathize with your kids and see things from their perspectives, you will probably find out they have been trying to convey their messages to you using any method to get your attention.

A labeling mindset will focus on the negatives. Some things you might think include:

- I had a terrible day.
- The kids are driving me crazy.
- My child is acting difficult as usual.
- My child didn't touch their food and wouldn't listen to what I said.
- Parenting is so difficult.
- Why does my child have to be so stubborn?

A positive mindset, on the other hand, will focus on the things that went well. A positive mindset doesn't dwell on the things that didn't go well:

- It's okay for my kids to act out; they're also human.
- Today didn't go as planned, but it wasn't all that bad because we got to spend quality time together.
- Although he didn't eat his lunch, he did finish his breakfast. Let's prepare for a nice dinner.
- Parenting is not all butterflies and flowers, but it balances out when I see my kids looking so happy and healthy.

Unfortunately, a label is a barrier that keeps you from parenting your child from a place of love, kindness, and empathy. A positive mindset will make your parenting journey memorable and keep you happy.

Practicing happy parenting doesn't mean you won't be correcting your child's misconduct. It means you won't use harsh punishments or put labels on your kids. Instead, you'll act to fulfill your child's emotional needs through a more refined approach such as positive interaction, which can nip bad behaviors in the bud.

A positive parenting mindset is like the icing on the cake of happy parenting!

> "Keep your face to the sunshine and you cannot see a shadow."
> —Helen Keller

Chapter 12

It's Not Too Late

"The bad news is time flies. The good news is you're the pilot."
- Michael Altshuler

"Oh, I really want things to be different, but my kids are already close to their teenage years. I think it's too late to make a difference.

Can you relate to the worries of this mother? Do her worries sound like yours? Sometimes, it's your thinking that limits you and leads to wrong assumptions. Perhaps you've already learned that 90% of whom you become as an adult is a result of your experiences over the first seven years of your life. Wouldn't it be a cruel twist of nature if inexperience were the only thing that had a significant impact on your child? Thankfully, that's not the case. Even if you've made a few mistakes along the way, your kids have picked up some good traits from you.

I've spoken to many parents who have confirmed that they want to spend time with their kids, be there for them, have a loving relationship with them, and feel connected to them. However, so many things get in the way that make them feel disconnected from their kids over time. Considering their kids' age, parents often think a reset is hard.

Luckily, recent studies have suggested that while early years count, later years shouldn't be ignored. This time period also matters. Brain plasticity continues throughout life, and kids can still learn regardless of their age. This means that no matter your child's age, it's never too late to work on your parenting style.

Parenting With Fewer Regrets

Perhaps, you think it's too late to make any notable difference in your kid's life because you've been yelling, swearing, and spanking them for many years. You believe you can't change anymore and lose hope, assuming there is no way to make things right anymore. But you're forgetting something – the fact that you're reading this book already shows that you want to parent differently. And guess what? It's not too late to do that!

There are many reasons why you're parenting the way you do. For example, you might have less support from family and friends than others have. You might feel stressed if you didn't have a good parenting model while growing up. Your parenting difficulty can also be due to a lack of experience, and you simply don't know how to handle difficult situations better.

Even though you started your parenting journey not believing in or caring about connection, it's never too late to do the necessary work. You can go back and start from the beginning. Not the beginning of your child's life because we don't have a time machine of course, but you can go to the beginning of the parenting process. Trust me, it's not too late to start.

Things You Can Start Doing TODAY!

The following are things you can start doing today to be a better parent.

- **Be Attachment-Minded**

We've already discussed attachment in Chapters 3 and 4 of this book, but it's still worth mentioning again. Being attachment-minded doesn't mean you have to follow a do's and don'ts list. Being attachment-minded isn't about the practices you followed or didn't follow when your child was an infant; it's about your mindset. Perhaps you're already attachment-minded without even realizing it. But as soon as you know you are wired to connect with your child, you can parent better. While it is called "attachment parenting," I choose to call it just "parenting." Think about it. Who wouldn't want to be close to their kids? I'm guessing no one.

Kids who have experienced insecure attachment from their parents have been hurt in many ways. However, it doesn't mean the past will determine the future. Instead, you can start focusing on nurturing a connection with your child now, not tomorrow. Over time, your child will likely grow up to be an independent, secure, and empathetic grownup.

Being attachment-minded doesn't mean you must be perfect or stay attuned to your kids 24/7. Instead, it means you accept your child is their own person and tuned into their needs. You should empathize with your child's experience and prioritize "being there" for them.

* * *

- **Create Remarkable Moments**

Wouldn't it be interesting to start each day with a new setting? Regardless of your child's age – whether toddler or teenager- you can begin to create sweet memories together every day. Of course, it will take time to create and foster those treasured moments, but ensure you make deliberate choices to spend time together. You can do activities such as walking around the neighborhood, eating meals, cleaning the house, shopping for groceries, and doing DIY projects together. Through these everyday activities, you can quickly create remarkable moments.

While doing mundane tasks, you can generously share your time and enjoy each cherished moment with your kids. Look around you and see where you can start. The kitchen is a great place to spend time because you can bake cookies or cakes, stuff turkeys, or make homemade ice cream for birthdays and holidays. There doesn't need to be a special occasion to do any of these activities. You can cook together any weekend. Trust me, your kids will look forward to bonding with you at the kitchen table. Use mealtime experience to create memories that will last a long time.

Other parents, including some dads, may want to play ball with their child, do puzzles together, play with musical instruments (even simple ones like egg shakers) or engage in "messy" play with sand, dirt, mud, water, clay, snow, etc. I know it will be a nightmare to clean up. But it's so good for their development!

Even when you don't have time to spare, you can allow your kids to tag along when you're running errands or on business trips if possible. If your work is flexible and allows kids around, it's also a good idea to bring them with you sometimes. These precious opportunities will help build rapport between you and your child, making conversations easier.

- **Be More Intentional with Your Kids**

I hear many parents say they regret not being more intentional with their kids. You tend to raise your kids as you were raised unless you make a conscious effort to be different. If you come from a family that doesn't care about taking family vacations frequently, you will model the same behavior with your kids. You might say things like, "Someday we'll go on that vacation we've been talking about," but in reality, you probably won't because life gets in the way.

Be active with your kids, even if you are exhausted after a long day at work. Go to that park, movie theater or museum. Take that vacation. You don't need to go on an expensive cruise or to Disneyland. Something simple like going camping or spending the day at the beach will do. You only have eighteen summer vacations with your kids before they become adults. Your "someday" plans won't happen unless you're intentional. Don't regret all the missed opportunities after your kids are grown.

Letters from Your Child

As parents, we already know what we want, but have we thought about what our children want? Just like we want our kids to be good and loving, they also have things they want from us. That includes spending time with us, their parents.

Kids want undivided attention when they spend time with their parents. They want their parents to listen and actually hear them. They want to be respected as kids and want their opinions to count without being corrected every time. Kids see their parents as the most precious and important people in their lives, just as parents treasure their kids.

We've all been kids at one point in our lives, but we have probably forgotten what it was like for us. I've tried to imagine being in my child's shoes, asking myself, *"If I were a child again, what would I love to tell my parents?"* I remember wishing my parents didn't act in certain ways. I also wanted them to know what I really wanted from them. Try and look into the hearts of your kids to understand what they want. Here are some things your child may want you to do:

1. **Take me seriously.**

I don't want you to make fun of me or downplay important things to me. Don't make jokes at my expense or consider my thoughts "cute." They may seem childish to you, but with my current knowledge and limited experience, this is how I perceive the world and think. Don't make fun of me if it's incorrect. Teach me what's right instead.

2. **Kindly respect my interests.**

I know I am a kid, but there's a reason I enjoy the things I do. So, allow me to show you why and what I love, whether it's playing video games, building with Legos, or making paper planes. You don't have to agree with or like it, but at least you'll know why it interests me, and perhaps you'll understand me better.

3. **Allow me to teach you things.**

I understand you're more knowledgeable and experienced than I am. But no matter how little I am, I also have knowledge and experience to share. Discussing my perspectives and new ideas will help broaden my horizons and clarify things. Teaching you something new will make me proud. Allow me to show you how deep or shallow my knowledge is without interrupting or making light of my thoughts.

4. **Don't interrupt me when possible**.

I would appreciate it if you respected my time, even though I'm a kid. I know I can't always have my way, but you should know that interrupting my creative moments, gameplay, or quiet time is really irritating. It can throw off my train of thought. My brain is learning to concentrate for long stretches and focus on tasks. Please let me finish if there's no reason to interrupt my work or thoughts.

5. **Allow me to make decisions for myself.**

Although I need to rely on you for important decisions and many other things I can't do alone, not having a say in my life is overly limiting. Allow me to have enough say in my life to give me a sense of responsibility and to make meaningful contributions to my life purpose. For example, I love choosing my outfit for the day in the color I love. I also like solving problems I can handle without help.

6. **Get to know and understand me**.

It's not right to try and mold me into who and how you think I should be. Instead, you should get to know me, and you will better understand who I already am. I am also discovering myself, so help me do this. Let's get to know me.

7. **Give me time and attention.**

I need your time and attention, so don't make me go the extra mile to get noticed by you. I don't want to act crazy, naughty, or get into fights to get your attention so you interact with me. Give me time and attention like you give to other things and people!

8. **Hold me.**

I want you to hold me physically and figuratively. I want to feel your hugs and affection. I need the security of your hands holding me and telling me everything is all right. I love it when you play with me and show me the right way to do things when I make mistakes. Although too much is not healthy, too little is equally bad.

It took me a few years to realize what kids want from their parents. I don't know about you, but whenever I see this list, it brings a smile to my face. It takes me back to my childhood and reminds me how I wanted many of these same things.

We can afford the things that make our children feel loved and cared for because the things they want and long for are not difficult or expensive.

The small things we do as parents make all the difference and mean the most to our kids. It is never too late to start and get things on the right track.

Conclusion

I am so proud of you. Well done!

You've done an incredible job staying with me from the beginning of this book to this point – the end. I hope you've enjoyed the experience just as I have. As we wrap up this journey, ensure that what you've learned so far reflects in your actions. Stay connected to your child from this point forward. But before I leave you, I have a few more words.

"Parents are the window to the world. Kids see the world through this window. Some of these windows shake from even the slightest wind. Other windows have broken glass. But good windows are strong and protect you from the cold and wind."

This is one of my favorite expressions, and I always recite it to remind myself how responsible I should be for my son. As windows to our kids' world, we must remain strong and ensure the window is clean to help them see the world safely.

I understand that you might struggle with your little ones, and things may not go as you imagined. But don't beat yourself up. It's all part of the parenting journey. Regardless of how your journey turns out, always seek a connection with your kids. Connection is the way to your child's heart and can prevent many problems with the child. Connection gets your child to listen to you, improving your bond.

Do you think you need to make huge improvements to feel connected to your child? I don't think so. Taking gradual steps is all that matters. Sometimes, your effort to build a connection with your child may seem unnoticed. You may think you're wasting your time. But even though your effort seems unnoticed, it's still meaningful. Over time, you'll see the unbelievably big difference in the relationship you have with your child.

Let's look at it from the perspective of someone on a diet. Being on a diet for a few days won't make you lose twenty pounds. However, if you remain consistent, you'll definitely see significant changes in your body. The point here is even though the results aren't visible in the early stages, there will be significant changes over time. Don't return to your old self or get discouraged when you don't notice change right away. Like all good things in life, connection takes time.

Also, if you feel disconnected from your child and blame yourself for not being the perfect parent, you need to stop feeling that way. Trust me, I've also been there, and it's not a good feeling. But acknowledging a problem and taking proactive steps to solve that problem is the way to go. That is exactly what I did, and I am here to tell you that you can bounce back and pick up from where you left off. I don't want parents to suffer like my old naïve self did, when I was parenting without paying attention to connection.

We can't deny the fact that parenting is a daily race. Do perfect parents and kids really exist in the end? I have never seen a perfect parent or a perfect kid, and I doubt that you have. We are all human and far from perfection. Being human comes with a lot of mess, but we need to know when we're wrong and when we're right. This knowledge helps us stay on the right course.

No doubt, kids grow up so fast. At one moment, you're dealing with the cries of your ten-month-old baby, and before you can even catch your breath, you already have a two-year-old toddler rolling on the floor. But it doesn't stop there because, in a few years, you'll have a child blowing out nine candles on their cake for their birthday. And then it's the teenage years. Wow! Already halfway through adulthood. Time really flies!

Once they're eighteen, you'll probably be officially fired from the role of active parent and rehired as a consultant. This is when your children are old enough to marry and vote. You'll probably be dropping them off at the college this time, too.

How do you picture the day you drop your child off at college? Do you want to look back and be proud of yourself for spending time with your child and appreciating the bond you've formed over the years? Or do you want to sob as you suddenly realize how much you've missed out on your child's life, knowing that time is up? I am hoping that with this book as your guide, you will look back and smile, grateful for the connection you've built with your kids. You'll be certain that you'll always be close throughout your lives, even though your child's on a new path.

Now that you have the time, make your house a home. Ask yourself, *how does your home feel right now? Is it conducive enough to make connection thrive?* Hopefully, your home is filled with love, peace, contentment, and security for your little ones. But if it is cluttered with chaos, I hope his book gives you a better idea of how to start fixing your home environment.

Start making yourself available to your child and act as their 24/7 support system. Even when you don't have all the answers to their problems, show them support, and together you can seek solutions to overcome the obstacles. The solution you find may not always be cut and dry, but what's important is that you're always available to help.

Finally, if you want to be a better parent, you need to practice, practice, practice. As I leave you, your new mantra should be **Read – Internalize – Execute.**

If you've gained valuable knowledge and enjoyed reading this book, kindly leave a review to let struggling parents know that there's hope and that it's never too late to start connecting with their kids. This book can be a good start for them as they work toward building an amazing connection with their kids.

Relax, parents, and take heart — the best is yet to come!

Please Review My Book
You Can Make A Difference

I'm truly delighted that you read my book. I hope it helps as a fellow parent. Your review will mean the world to me and keep me on my journey to help others.
I appreciate your help.

References

Ballinger, B. (n.d). 6 Ways To Know That You Are A Good Parent (And 6 Ways You Can Improve). Retrieved from https://parentingthemodernfamily.com/6-ways-know-good-parent-6-ways-can-improve/

Banks, C. (n.d). Disrespectful Child Behavior? Don't Take It Personally. Retrieved from https://www.empoweringparents.com/article/disrespectful-child-behavior-dont-take-it-personally/

Bharatan, N. (2020, November). 26 House Rules For Kids And Tips To Help Them Follow. Retrieved from https://www.momjunction.com/articles/house-rules-for-kids-list_00763041/

Borelli, J.L & Lai, J. (2019, June). How to Decipher the Emotions Behind Your Child's Behaviors. Retrieved from https://greatergood.berkeley.edu/article/item/how_to_decipher_the_emotions_behind_your_childs_behaviors

BUGK.org. (n.d). Understanding Yourself As A Parent. Retrieved from http://www.bringingupgreatkids.org/en/parenthood/understanding-yourself-as-a-parent

Centers for Disease Control and Prevention. (2019, November). Creating Rules. Retrieved from https://www.cdc.gov/parents/essentials/structure/rules.html

Child Guidance Resource Centers. (October, 2020). Parenting Strategies: The Benefits of House Rules. Retrieved from https://cgrc.org/blog/parenting-strategies-the-benefits-of-house-rules/

Coverthree. (n.d). Kids Brain Development: the Factors & Stages That Shape Kids' Brain. Retrieved from https://coverthree.com/blogs/research/kids-brain-development

ECLKC. (n.d). News You Can Use: Early Experiences Build the Brain. Retrieved from https://eclkc.ohs.acf.hhs.gov/school-readiness/article/news-you-can-use-early-experiences-build-brain

First Thing First, (n.d). Brain Development. Retrieved from https://www.firstthingsfirst.org/early-childhood-matters/brain-development/

Garcia, N. (2022, May). On Accepting Your Children for Who They Are. Retrieved from https://sleepingshouldbeeasy.com/accepting-your-children/

Gillies, B. (2022, October) 50 Easy Ways to Be a Fantastic Parent. Retrieved from https://www.parents.com/parenting/better-parenting/advice/ways-to-be-fantastic-parent/

Glembocki, V. (2022, January). How to Stop Yelling at Your Kids—and What to Do

Instead. Retrieved from https://www.parents.com/parenting/better-parenting/advice/how-to-quit-yelling-at-your-kids/

Harris, B. (n.d). Have You Accepted the Child You've Got? Retrieved from https://bonnieharris.com/accepted-child-youve-got-2/

HMG Org. (n.d). How to Encourage a Child's Brain Development. Retrieved from https://helpmegrowmn.org/HMG/HelpfulRes/Articles/HowEncourageBrainDev/index.html

Holmes, K. (n.d). The Best Questions to Ask Your Kid Instead of "How Was Your Day?" Retrieved from https://happyyouhappyfamily.com/questions-for-kids/

Hurley, K. (2019, February). 10 Positive Parenting Mantras to Help You Stay Calm. Retrieved from https://ourdailymess.com/2019/02/26/10-positive-parenting-mantras-to-channel-your-inner-calm/

Karp, H. (n.d). How to Discipline a Toddler. Retrieved from https://www.happiestbaby.com/blogs/toddler/when-does-discipline-begin

Keston, V. (2013, November). Finding a Middle Ground: Six Ways to Give Our Children Room to Grow without Undue Risk. Retrieved from https://gooseling.com/middle-ground-parenting/

Kids Helpline. (n.d). Helping kids identify and express feelings. Retrieved from https://kidshelpline.com.au/parents/issues/helping-kids-identify-and-express-feelings

Kolitz, D. (2018, September). Do Kids Feel Stronger Emotions Than Adults? Retrieved from https://gizmodo.com/do-kids-feel-stronger-emotions-than-adults-1828933152

Krisbergh, A. (n.d). Being A Role Model – The Promise And The Peril. Retrieved from https://centerforparentingeducation.org/library-of-articles/focus-parents/role-model-promise-peril/

Kwan, E. (2017, September). Ten Ways to Connect With Your Child Everyday. Retrieved from https://www.handinhandparenting.org/2017/09/10-ways-to-connect-with-your-child-everyday/

Lansbury, J. (n.d). If Gentle Discipline Isn't Working, This Might Be the Reason. Retrieved from https://www.janetlansbury.com/2012/10/if-gentle-discipline-isnt-working-this-might-be-the-reason/

Lehman, J. (n.d). Parent the Child You Have, Not the Child You Wish You Had. Retrieved from https://www.empoweringparents.com/article/parent-child-you-have/

Leo, P. (n.d). Connecting Through Filling the Love Cup. Retrieved from https://www.naturalchild.org/articles/pam_leo/love_cup.html

Li, P. (2022, October). Discipline vs Punishment: The Difference In Child Development. Retrieved from https://www.parentingforbrain.com/discipline-vs-punishment/

Li, P. (2022, October). How To Get Kids To Listen. Retrieved from https://www.parentingforbrain.com/how-to-get-kids-to-listen/

Li, P. (2022, November). Controlling Parents – 20 Signs And Why They Are Harmful. Retrieved from https://www.parentingforbrain.com/controlling-parents/

Loewen, M. (2007, January). Am I a Good Parent? Retrieved from https://launchpad-counseling.com/blog/parent-coaching/am-i-a-good-parent/

MacGregor, J. (2020, March). How to fill your child's emotional cup. Retrieved from https://funmammasa.co.za/how-to-fill-your-childs-emotional-cup/

Markham, L. (2016, December). What's Connection Parenting? Q and A. retrieved from https://www.ahaparenting.com/read/connection-parenting-Q-A

McCready, A. (n.d). How to Get Kids to (REALLY) Listen: 7 Steps for Success. Retrieved from https://www.positiveparentingsolutions.com/parenting/get-kids-to-listen

McGuinness, D. (2022, August). 6 Small Ways to Make Each of Your Kids Feel Special. Retrieved from https://www.parents.com/parenting/better-parenting/advice/6-small-ways-to-make-each-of-your-kids-feel-special/

Meinke, H. (2019, December). Understanding the Stages of Emotional Development in Children. Retrieved from https://www.rasmussen.edu/degrees/education/blog/stages-of-emotional-development/

Messy Yet Lovely. (n.d). How to connect with your child and build a great relationship. Retrieved from https://workingparenting.com/connection-before-correction/

Morgenstein, J. (n.d). It's Never Too Late To Hit Reset With Your Kids. Retrieved from https://www.juliemorgenstern.com/tips-tools-blog/2020/1/23/its-never-too-late-to-hit-reset-with-your-kids

Morin, A. (2021, January). Role Model the Behavior You Want to See From Your Kids. Retrieved from https://www.verywellfamily.com/role-model-the-behavior-you-want-to-see-from-your-kids-1094785

Morin, A. (2022, September). 5 Types of Household Rules Kids Need. Retrieved from https://www.verywellfamily.com/types-of-rules-kids-need-1094871

Morin, A. (2022, October). A Sample of Family Household Rules. Retrieved from https://www.verywellfamily.com/examples-of-household-rules for the entire-family-1094879

Nelson, J. (n.d). Connection Before Correction. Retrieved from https://www.positivediscipline.com/articles/connection-correction-0

Nikki, C.T. 2020, November). 10 Reasons Why Moms Cry. Retrieved from https://fairfieldcounty.momcollective.com/moms-cry-reasons-why/

Pace, R. (2022, February). 25 Ways on How to Be a Better Parent. Retrieved from https://www.marriage.com/advice/parenting/ways-to-be-a-better-parent/

Parenting From Scratch. (2013, October). When Is it Too Late to Build a Secure Attachment With My Child? Retrieved from https://parentingfromscratch.wordpress.com/2013/10/23/when-is-it-too-late-to-build-a-secure-attachment-with-my-child/

Plugarasu, M. (2022, May). Connection in Parenting: Back to Basics. Retrieved from https://mihaelaplugarasu.com/connection-in-parenting-back-to-basics/

Practice Notes. (2014, July). Why Attachment Matters. Retrieved from https://practicenotes.org/v19n3/matters.htm

Rogers, R. (n.d). Parenting with no regrets before it's too late. Retrieved from https://www.focusonthefamily.ca/content/parenting-with-no-regrets-before-its-too-late

Rueter, A. (n.d). When Mom and Dad have Different Parenting Styles. Retrieved from https://messymotherhood.com/when-mom-and-dad-have-different-parenting-styles-2/

Simply Rooted Family. (2022, June). How to Adjust Your Body Language When Talking to Your Kids to Speak Love. Retrieved from https://simplyrootedfamily.com/2020/06/22/love-language-for-kids/

Stasney, S. (n.d). 4 Simple But Effective Ways For Connecting With Your Child. Retrieved from https://www.thisnthatparenting.com/connecting-with-your-child/

Taylor, E. (2022, July). Moms Have Feelings Too. Retrieved from https://fairfieldcounty.momcollective.com/moms-have-feelings-too/

The Consciously Parenting Project. (n.d). 4 things you can do today when you feel disconnected from your child. Retrieved from https://consciouslyparenting.com/blog/4-things-when-disconnected/

The Foundations for Learning Center. (n.d). The Importance of Unconditional Love. Retrieved from https://www.thefoundationforlearning.com/child-care/the-importance-of-unconditional-love/

The Pragmatic Parent. (n.d). Parenting Mindset: How You See Your Child on Hard Days Affects Your Relationship. Retrieved from https://www.thepragmaticparent.com/parenting-mindset-positive-parenting-connection/

UNICEF. (n.d) How to discipline your child the smart and healthy way. Retrieved from https://www.unicef.org/parenting/child-care/how-discipline-your-child-smart-and-healthy-way

Working Parenting. (2016, July). 3 Easy Ways to "Connect Before Correct" in parenting. Retrieved from https://workingparenting.com/connection-before-correction/

Printed in Great Britain
by Amazon